The Autobiography of Brantley York

The Autobiography of Brantley York

Brantley York

THE AUTOBIOGRAPHY OF BRANTLEY YORK

By

BRANTLEY YORK

DURHAM, N. C.
THE SEEMAN PRINTERY
1910

HISTORIC PUBLISHING
SAN ANTONIO, TEXAS
All Rights Reserved
©2017

CONTENTS

- Preface 10
- Introductory Sketch 11
- CHAPTER I.

Birth--Extraordinary Snow--Parentage--Family 19

- CHAPTER II.

Ancestry 20

- CHAPTER III.

Boyhood--Early Education--Religious Impressions--Ignorance and Superstitions of the Bush Creek Neighborhood 22

- CHAPTER IV.

My Father Involved in Debt--Property Sold--Family Scattered 29

- CHAPTER V.

Removal of the Family 32

- CHAPTER VI.

The Moral Conditions of the Neighborhood--A Young Lady Converted at a Dance Frolic--A Revival of Religion 36

- CHAPTER VII.

The Family Removes--Engages in Farming--First Camp Meeting--Conviction and Conversion 38

- CHAPTER VIII.

Secret Prayer--Class Meetings--Band Meetings 41

- CHAPTER IX.

1824-1837--Camp Meetings--The Ministry--Teaching 44

- CHAPTER X.

The Origin of Trinity College 60

- CHAPTER XI.

Clemonsville--Itinerant Teaching--Olin High School--Blindness--Career as Author--York Collegiate Institute 65

- CHAPTER XII.

The Commencement of the War 90

- CHAPTER XIII.

Third Year of the War-'63 93

- CHAPTER XIV.

Fourth Year of the War 96

- CHAPTER XV.
1865.
The End of the War--Unsettled State of Society and Scarceness of Provisions--School Taught at York Collegiate Institute--Two Sons in the War 97
- CHAPTER XVI.
1866. Traveling and Lecturing and Teaching Classes--At Snow Creek Camp Meeting and Sunday School Convention at Rock Spring 98
- CHAPTER XVII.
Classes Taught at Catawba Station--Three Camp Meetings Visited--A Preaching and Visiting Tour, Etc 99
- CHAPTER XVIII.
Logic Classes Taught at Statesville--Classes at Olin High School and in Salisbury--Preached in Three Different Places--Political Excitement--Colored Churches--Grammar Classes Taught in Statesville--A Visit to Major York's--Grammar Classes Taught in Chatham and Wake--Ruffin Badger Institute 101
- CHAPTER XIX.
Ruffin Badger Institute--Educational Association Organized--Teachers' Meeting Formed--Elected Professor in Rutherford College--Preparing "Man of Business" for Publication--Death of Fannie S. York--Organization of Local Ministers' Conference 104
- CHAPTER XX.
Lecturing Tour, Visiting Graham, N. C., Sylvian Academy, Mount Vernon Springs--Rutherford College Commencement--Class Taught at Columbia and Franklinsville Factories--Assumes the Duties of Professorship at Rutherford College 106
- CHAPTER XXI.
Begin Labor in Rutherford College as Professor and Agent--Teaching Side Classes--New College Building Erected--Lecturing in College on Social Law and Etiquette--Visiting Various Camp Meetings--Revival Among the Students--Resignation as Professor and Agent 107
- CHAPTER XXII.
Leaving for Arkansas--Arrival--Disappointment--Lecturing and Teaching Classes at Russellville--At Dardenville--At Athens--Lewisburg--Conway--Lone Oak--Arrival at Home 109

- CHAPTER XXIII.

Teaching and Lecturing at Rutherford College, Hickory and Morganton--An Eastern Tour--Sick at Newton--Lecturing and Preaching at Statesville--Mooresville--Sick at Davidson College--Preaching in Charlotte--At Monroe, etc.--In South Carolina, at Bennettsville--Teaching Classes at Gilboa, Pine Grove, Jerusalem--Return Home 114

- CHAPTER XXIV.

Teaching Logic and Grammar at the College--Reading Proofsheets at Mebanesville--Returning Home--Teaching at Mill Grove--Visiting Three Camp Meetings--Teaching and Lecturing at Bethel--At Home--Teaching Logic and Grammar--Returned to Bethel--Teaching at Mill Grove, at Mathews--Returned Home 120

- CHAPTER XXV.

Lecturing and Preaching Tour--Lecturing and Preaching at Newton, Catawba Station--Statesville--Lexington, Yadkin College--At Thomasville--Trinity College--Ebenezer--Randleman--Cedar Falls--Franklinsville--Mebanesville--Durham, Mooresville, etc-- 122

- CHAPTER XXVI.

A Western Tour--Preaching and Lecturing at Nebo--Marion--Old Fort--Asheville--Resting at Hon. R. B. Vance's--At Turkey Creek Camp and District Meeting--At Burnesville--Home. 126

- CHAPTER XVII.

North Carolina Conference--Prohibition Bill Presented to People--Lecturing on Prohibition, etc 128

- CHAPTER XXVIII.

Opening of New Salem and Randleman High School--Educational Association--Moving into the New Building--The School in a Flourishing Condition--Resignation of the Principal, Prof. Rheim, and Prof. York 132

- CHAPTER XXIX.

A Tour in South Carolina--Teaching Classes, Preaching and Lecturing--Publishing Common School Grammar--Thrown from a Buggy, Seriously Hurt--Visiting Children in Wake, Chatham and Orange Counties 136

- CHAPTER XXX.

Traveling for My Health--Greensboro--Reidsville--Leaksville--Home 139

- CHAPTER XXXI.

Tour to the Middle of the State--Teaching a Grammar Class at Morrisville--Lecturing and Teaching at Various Places--Protracted Meetings 141

- CHAPTER XXXII.

Prohibition Convention in Greensboro--Mebanesville--Teaching at New Salem--Take Charge of School at Fair View--Lecturing and Preaching--Dobson Circuit and Rocky Springs Camp Meeting 143

- CHAPTER XXXIII.

Golden Wedding--Dobson Circuit--Teaching, Lecturing, and Preaching--Brevard Circuit--Preaching--Visiting in Yancey and Buncombe--Visits in Stanley County 147

The Autobiography of Brantley York

PREFACE

In 1896 the Trinity College Historical Society established an Annual Publication of Historical Papers. Eight numbers have been issued, consisting of discussions before the Society and letters and documents which have come into its possession. The growth of the work and collections of the organization has suggested a new venture--the publication of memoirs, autobiographies and monographs in book form. These will not supplant the Historical Papers, but will be continuous with the publication already begun. Consequently the present volume is presented to the public. It will be followed in 1911 by the Memoirs of Governor W. W. Holden, later by Dr. E. W. Caruthers' Evils of American Slavery' and monographic studies.

The editorial difficulties involved in preparing Dr. York's autobiography for the press have been peculiar. He began his work in 1876, long after he became blind, and continued it at various intervals until 1888. The amanuenses to whom he dictated were not equally qualified for their task. Some were well educated; others barely knew the rudiments of orthography. Consequently, as the manuscript was never revised, there is no uniformity in the use of capitals and punctuation marks. In preparing the copy for the printer, some changes were found to be not only feasible, but almost necessary. But the aim has been to make the printed page correspond with the written. Errors in orthography should not reflect on the learning of Dr. York; rather they should give an impression of the limitations which beset him, and illustrate his greatest opportunity for service, viz.; teaching his fellow men the elements of English grammar.

Professor E. C. Brooks, of the Department of Education, has contributed the biographical sketch of Dr. York. Dr. W. T. Laprade, Assistant Professor of History, has aided in reading the proof.

WM. K. BOYD.

Trinity College, Durham, N. C., May 1, 1910.

INTRODUCTORY SKETCH

What our civilization would be today but for the old time preacher, it is hard to say. His tremendous faith and religious zeal may have filled his imagination with many realities that have no significance for the cold, practical, calculating eye of today; and judged by the standards of today he loses. But in pioneer days of nearly a century ago, when settlements were isolated and remote from culture and commercial activities; when the inbreeding of fatuous ideas was turning civilization back toward primitive man; when post offices, newspapers, literature, Sunday-schools and secular schools were unknown to vast wild areas; when Christianity was graded little higher than the animism of the Red-man, the old time preacher was the one, and about the only, apostle of enlightenment that the back districts heard, and his everlasting influence is felt. Wherever he went he preached a burning gospel, and the household gods of these hardy woodmen beamed with a simple truth. Wherever he hitched his horse and threw down his saddle-bags, he found a welcomed resting place, and the neighbors would follow a trail for miles leading to his abode, and sit the long night by the great open fire listening to the stories of the world beyond. Politics and commerce, men and measures, were his theme; and before the night grew still he would draw forth his New Testament and explain to the simple woodmen the still more simple plan of salvation. Such were his methods, and his coming and going, events of state importance, wove into their primitive lives some of the culture and the hope of the race until they became a part of the warp and woof of humanity.

What our civilization would be today but for the coming of the old time preacher, it is hard to say, but a picture of neglected and forgotten humanity can be imagined.

One of these apostles of enlightenment was the Reverend Brantley York, the blind teacher and preacher, whose autobiography tells of the labors of a century almost, and pictures the backwoodsman in his daily routine. The social, moral, religious and industrial life is given as the author tells the story of his own life from infancy to past his fourscore years.

The York family, natives of Yorkshire, England, came to America during the first half of the Eighteenth Century, and located in what is now Randolph County, where Brantley York was born. His grandfather and grandmother in their youth came over together in the same vessel, and shortly afterwards married. Eli York, the father of Brantley York, was only a lad in his teens when Cornwallis made his headquarters at Salem. He was a frequent visitor to the American camp, carrying clothes and rations to his brothers. He had started on such an errand when he heard the guns at the battle of Guilford Court House. Meeting the wounded and the stragglers fleeing from the battle, and being frightened by the reports brought from the army, the lad turned back, carrying his supplies with him.

Eli York became a miner, and he was something of a rude chemist in those days. In the Second War of Independence, 1812-15, he was employed by the U. S. Government to manufacture gunpowder. Brantley, then a small lad, went with the laborers who traversed Randolph and Guilford counties raking dirt from under tobacco barns, from which saltpetre was obtained; and many a day, with a home-made knife, he cut the gourds in which the powder was stored, then transferred by the wagon-load to the army magazine.

The York home was located on Bush Creek, in Randolph County. Here Brantley York, the seventh son, was born January 3, 1805. From his father he inherited his mining propensities, and in early life was connected with several mining ventures, none of which turned out profitably.

In those days educational facilities were very poor. Many communities knew not the school, and many a child never saw a schoolmaster. Young Brantley, however, more fortunate, entered school at four years of age, to be frightened out of his wits by an old master who kept thrashing the floor to terrify the young. Master Short passed into his life a few years later, and his only contract bound him to abstain from drinking during school hours, yet he was not forbidden to sleep away in the schoolroom the fumes of a midnight debauch; for Master Short was a confirmed drunkard. At eight years of age young Brantley did pass under the touch of a real schoolmaster, and he was taught "to spell in five syllables," and at the end of one term he "acted a part of a dialogue." When he was able to read the New Testament he was put in

* to see p. 7.

writing, "for in those days no one thought of putting one in writing till he could read the New Testament."

At thirteen his school days ended. His father having lost all his property Brantley was "hired out." The family moved about from place to place, and finally the lad found a home near the old location of Trinity College in Randolph County. He received here not only employment, but kindness and encouragement.

In those days every man who owned his land had his whiskey still. Even at the early age of five young Brantley knew the ways of the still. He played with the beverage as it dropped from the worm, and more than once did he feel its influence in his boyhood days. Both preacher and layman took their morning drams, and the alphabet hardly contained letters arranged sufficiently to spell Temperance Society.

Many of those back settlements were in almost total ignorance of the God of the New Testament. Demon worship, with its chief attribute, witchcraft, held the spiritual life in mortal terror. Goblins and hobgoblins, ghosts and spooks, visible only to the hypersensitive, and audible everywhere to the terrified, brought back to earth a hybrid animism, showing faint traces of a more cheerful Christianity. Their agents in the flesh were the fortune-teller and the conjure-doctor. Young Brantley, being an emotional and excitable lad was dragged before these important high-priests of superstition; and he heard the predictions from Old Bass, famous in the occult sciences: "He will end his ignominious career on the gallows;" and he was frequently reminded in his younger days that "Old Bass' predictions are coming true."

When Young Brantley was not yet a man, Randolph County was a part of the Deep River Circuit of the South Carolina Conference. This will give one some idea of the labors of the old time circuit rider and the frequency of his visits. The first Methodist minister to visit the neighborhood of the Yorks was Christenberg.

* Christenberry, see p. 7.

Although the Yorks were Primitive Baptists, the coming of Christenberg and the era of revivals and camp-meetings produced many changes. Ebenezer Church, near Old Trinity, was established. Soon Young Brantley was converted. Here a library society was organized. Into this went Young

Brantley's spare earnings; and through it he laid the foundation of his education and ministerial career.

Although a hired boy, working here and there, the little library at Ebenezer Church gave him an opportunity. After the day's work, he read and studied by the light of pine knots. He soon mastered arithmetic and became a neighborhood celebrity. He wrote a beautiful hand, an accomplishment which excited the admiration of youth and old age in the community.

At the age of nineteen, he was converted at a camp-meeting at Ebenezer Church, and in 1831, at the age of twenty-six, he was licensed to preach. He was twenty-four years old and married, when he saw his first English grammar; and he immediately set to work to master it. So he did with Latin, Greek, the higher mathematics, natural philosophy, logic and rhetoric. The year he was licensed to preach he began teaching. Within a few years his fame as a teacher had risen and he was known as one who could teach geometry, trigonometry, surveying, Coesar, Virgil, and could read the New Testament in Greek.

It seems that blindness was hereditary in the family. His only recollection of his grandfather was a picture of the old gentleman in total blindness, and "I remember standing between his knees while he passed his hands over my face and head." Although he had barely reached middle life when he likewise lost his sight, yet the best part of his life was worked out in almost total darkness.

This blind preacher-teacher was a unique figure. His very active career stretched almost across the Nineteenth Century, and there is hardly a county in the State that did not at some time furnish him a congregation or a school. He was always active. Sometimes alone, sometimes with his wife, sometimes with daughter or son, he traveled the State and preached with earnestness and power the duty of parents both in religion and in education.

For more than fifty years he taught and preached. The story of those camp-meeting days has gone into history. Tremendous waves of religious fervor, midnight sermons, wrestling all night with the forces of evil, going days without food--these are deeds that belong to the pioneer days of church history; and it is this history that Brantley York has recorded in his Autobiography.

In education he was a real circuit rider. It is probable that Brantley York organized more schools than any other man in America. In the villages and in the backwoods, in log cabins and in churches, in parlors and in hotels, in farms and under clear skies, he organized his grammar classes. From Morehead City to Asheville, from Columbia, S. C., to Danville, Va., in Tennessee and Arkansas, he taught youth and old age the principles of the mother tongue. He wrote his own books and published them at his own expense; and wherever a congregation could be formed he was either preaching the gospel or teaching York's grammar. And these things he was doing in his eighty-sixth year, when the order came to rest.

When a young man he resolved to end the drink habit, which had almost claimed him as a victim, and long before the Civil War he was organizing temperance societies and lecturing on the evils of strong drink; and in 1881 in his 76th year, when the State first moved toward prohibition, he lectured in almost every county.

Brantley York worked in his own way. He never joined the conference, but always styled himself a local preacher. He organized many academies, but he never worked in any organization long. Union Institute, which he organized, became Trinity College, but it was his successor that saw the college grow out of the high school. Here he lost the sight of one eye.

Clemmonsville High School, in Davidson County, had great prosperity under his management. He formed Olin High School and here he lost his other eye; later he became principal of York Collegiate Institute; in 1869 he was elected principal of Ruffin-Badger Institute, where he labored with much success until he was called to Rutherford College as professor of logic and rhetoric. In 1881 he, with his son, Rev. B. A. York, formed New Salem and Randleman High School, in Randolph County, and after teaching there with his son for four years, he left the teaching profession, never to return to it again. His career as author of text-books is told in Chapter XI of the Autobiography. After his death, an edition of the High School Grammar was published, in 1894, by Dr. L. Branson, of North Carolina, and by Prof. F. P. Julian of Peoria, Ill., who now owns the copyright to his books.

For more than seventy years he was a teacher and preacher. He had under his tuition more than 15,000 pupils; and he himself estimated that he had preached and lectured more than 8,000 times. At no time was he idle.

Even the last six weeks of his life he preached more than a dozen times, aiding his son Rev. B. A. York in a revival on the Forest City Circuit; and on October 7, 1891, at the age of eighty-six years, the order came for him to rest.

Rutherford College, the institution at which he labored, conferred on him the degree of Doctor of Divinity. His appreciative students, numbering many thousands, erected a beautiful monument over his grave at York Institute, where he was buried.

No greater evidence can we have of a man's great sincerity than this, that the children choose the father's profession and labor with the same zeal and earnestness. I have before me a newspaper clipping of much length, telling of a service where the father and two sons occupied the pulpit the same day, one in the morning, the other in the afternoon, and the father at night. We have no finer picture of devotion to duty than the blind father led about by his son, both preaching the gospel, or teaching the youth of the land.

Dr. Brantley York was a man of very fine appearance. He was six feet two inches tall, of blue eyes and fair skin, very erect, and weighed about 200 pounds. He was a man of indomitable will, but considerate and kind. He was twice married. His first wife was Rachel Sherwood, of Guilford County, by whom he had two children. Both of these are dead. Mary W. Lineberry, of Randolph County was his second wife. She is still living and is in her ninety-first year. By her he had eleven children. Of these six are dead and seven are living.

The seven surviving children are thus located: Mrs. Jennie Rheim, of Butte, Montana. Her husband, Capt. J. E. Rheim was a professor in Weaverville College ten years. Here he died. Rev. D. V. York, D. D., is a member of the Holston Conference; Rev. B. A. York, A. M., is a member of the Western North Carolina Conference. W. B. York is a lawyer, teacher and farmer, and lives at Mebane, N. C.; N. D. York is a practicing physician at Mebane; W. C. York is a farmer, and lives at Taylorsville, N. C.; Mrs. Nora Clontz, wife of W. J. Clontz, M. D., lives at Alexander, Buncombe County, N. C.

The following sons and daughters are dead: Maj. Richard W. York, a practicing attorney of Chatham County; Fannie S. York; Rachel L. York, wife of T. F. Elliotte; Lucretia York and Amos W. York.

Hundreds of people are living today who remember most affectionately the blind preacher-teacher who tells here the story of his own life. Many hundreds more are living who have been influenced by the children of the blind preacher-teacher, and can testify feelingly that their works do follow them.

E. C. BROOKS.

Trinity College, Durham, N. C.

BRANTLEY YORK

THE AUTOBIOGRAPHY OF BRANTLEY YORK

CHAPTER I.

BIRTH--EXTRAORDINARY SNOW--PARENTAGE--FAMILY.

I was born in Randolph County, N. C. January 3, 1805, on a small stream called Bush Creek, some six miles north of Franklinsville. At that time one of the deepest snows ever known in that section of the state had fallen some two weeks previous to my birth, its average depth being about thirty-six inches.

I was the son of Eli and Susanna York the seventh of nine children; of these five were males, viz, Harden, Hiram, William, Brantley and John Wesley and four females, Polly (Mary), Hannah, Sallie and Jemima. Two of the brothers Harden and Hiram are dead. Harden, the oldest brother, died in the State of Indiana some thirty-four or thirty-five years ago. Hiram died in the eastern portion of this state since the war. The circumstances of his death [are] not known.

One Sister, Sallie (Mrs. Aydlott) died in Guilford County some twelve years since. Her husband, Benjamin Aydlott survived her but a short time. Polly (Mrs. Coltrane) the oldest child, is still living, being about eighty-three years of age. My sister Hannah (Mrs. Bond) removed to the State of Missouri nearly forty years ago; whether living or dead is to me unknown, but I have learned that her husband, Mr. John Bond is dead. My youngest Sister, the youngest of the family, Mrs. Jemima Mendenhall since the War removed to the State of Indiana. When heard from last she was living.

I was named for a Baptist preacher,--the Rev. William Brantley, of Chatham County, subsequently Doctor (D. D.) of Charleston, S. C.

My parents, either before or soon after I was born, heard the Rev. W. Brantley preach at a church called Millstone in Randolph County, and were so well pleased with him as a man and as a preacher that they gave me his family name (Brantley) and I should have received the other but from the fact that I had an older brother named William.

CHAPTER II.

ANCESTRY.

According to tradition, many years ago a man by the name of York came from Yorkshire, England, and settled in this State on Sandy Creek and from this man the numerous family of the Yorks originated, and are now scattered throughout many of the states of the Union. My Grandfather, Henry York, lived and died on Sandy Creek (Randolph County). He was blind,-- totally blind for several years before his death. I have only a faint recollection of him, and about the only thing recollected is that when very small I remember standing between his knees while he passed his hands over my face and head, it being the only means by which he could form any idea of me, as he was then blind. My father had several brothers, the most of whom were older than himself. I believe he was the youngest of the first set of children; for his father was married twice; and I recollect having seen one only of the last children. But I have a clear recollection of having seen three of my paternal uncles viz, Samuel, William and Edmund. My father had some Sisters, but I have no recollection of any but one, viz., Mrs. Mollie Ruth. Many of her offspring are still living on Sandy Creek, Randolph County. But the whole family brothers and Sisters of my father, have long since passed away. My father died at the advanced age of eighty-four. And he, as well as my mother reposes in the graveyard of Ebenezer Church, Randolph County.

My father, perhaps before I was born, united himself with the (Primitive) Baptist denomination. He held his membership at Sandy Creek Church--one of the oldest Baptist churches in the State. But after he removed from that section of the State, he never attached himself to any other church, and was for several years in a back-slidden state; but some twenty or twenty-five years previous to his death, he joined the Temperance Society, and not long after was reclaimed, and from that time to the end of his earthly career, he lived a pious and devoted christian, and died in the triumphs of the Gospel faith.

My mother's family name was Harden. She was born in the State of Virginia, county not recollected, and when about fourteen years of age, her father removed from Virginia to North Carolina and settled on Sandy Creek, Randolph County.

My maternal Grandfather Mark Harden died before my recollection; but his widow Hannah Harden my maternal grandmother survived him several years; of her I have a distinct recollection, though she died when I was a small boy. Of the religious predilections of my maternal Grandparents I know nothing. My Grandmother's family name was Holder, if I am not mistaken. They left behind them several children, all of whom were daughters except one. Of these my mother was the oldest, and my maternal Uncle Mark Harden, junior, was the youngest.

I have a distinct recollection of three of my maternal Aunts; viz, Mrs. Polly Warren, Anna Holder, and Lettie Roache. All of these have passed away except Mrs. Holder. She, when last heard from, was living, and I suppose cannot be much less than one hundred years old.

My mother died in 1846, and was buried as has already been mentioned in the graveyard at Ebenezer church. She never attached herslf to any church, but was inclined most strongly toward the M. E. church. I have, however, good reasons for believing that for many years before her death she was a christian. Her walk was exemplary, and no one, perhaps, appreciated preaching more than she. She died as was supposed from the effects of paralysis, consequently, she said very little during her illness, but manifested a strong desire to see me before she died, but of this favor she was denied; for I was away from home when the news of her illness arrived, and when I reached my father's, she had been buried some two days.

My Uncle, Mark Harden, was a member of the M. P. Church for several years before his decease. His first wife (for he was married twice) Sarah York was a cousin of mine, the daughter of William York. She also was a member of the same church of her husband and died some eight or ten years before her husband. His second wife, of whom I know but little, is still living.

CHAPTER III.

BOYHOOD--EARLY EDUCATION--RELIGIOUS IMPRESSIONS--IGNORANCE AND SUPERSTITIONS OF THE BUSH CREEK NEIGHBORHOOD.

Twelve years of my boyhood were spent at the old homestead on Bush Creek. Like other boys, I was fond of sport. During the warm season I spent much time fishing with the bow and arrow, and during the cold season, trapping for birds.

For several years, I was much afflicted with erysipelas, then called St. Anthony's fire. The principal remedy resorted to was blood-letting. This, in my case, was so frequently resorted to that the very thought to my mind was horrifying; nor have I ever been entirely free from this feeling; for, while I have no great dred [sic] of suffering pain, yet the use of any surgical instrument is still the object of much dread.

When about five or six years old, an incident occurred which came very near terminating my life. My mother sent an older brother and me to call my father to breakfast. When we reached the Still-house, he was just starting what is called a "doubling" and could not leave. In the meantime I got behind the worm-tub and by the use of a spoon I found between the hoop and stave, I commenced catching the liquor, as it issued from the worm and drinking it; for I loved the taste of it, nor have I any recollection of any time previous to this when I did not; for I suppose I was like other babies, drenched with it by means of a teaspoon. As soon as discovered by my father, both brother and I were sent home, the distance being some three or four hundred yards. Well did the wise man say, "Wine is a mocker," for it made me believe I was what I was not, and that I could do what I could not; for, notwithstanding I was very feeble, yet I believed I could pull up any tree in the forest by the root, and so foolish was I that I actually tried it. After much stumbling and falling, I finally reached within some twenty-five or thirty yards of home, and there I fell, and from that time till the morning of the next day, I was as unconscious of everything around me as if I had been dead.

If mothers were aware of the danger of such a habit when formed, they would be extremely cautious in either giving their children ardent spirits as a beverage or a medicine; for, perhaps in every case of this kind, the remedy is worse than the disease.

At this time (1876) it may be thought strange that any member of the church should follow the distillation of ardent spirits as a livelyhood (sic) but the view entertained by even good people at the time of which I speak, were very different; for no one supposed it was wrong either to make or drink ardent spirits moderately; drunkenness only was regarded as a sin even by ministers.

Education during my boyhood was at an extremely low ebb, there being but very few schools, and they of a very low grade. The first school I attended I was only about four years old, and went only one day. I went not so much to learn as to be with a favorite sister who had been my nurse. The schoolmaster (as teachers were then called) was a very large, sour-looking man, and seemed to appreciate very highly the dignity of his position. And the instruments of punishment lay thick around him, in the form of switches and small paddles called ferrules, and among the switches was a very large and long one, kept for the purpose of thrashing the floor in order to frighten the urchins, and keep them in awe of his authority. But one was allowed to go out at a time, and in order to prevent the violation of this rule, a little hooked stick suspended to a peg or nail driven in the door-facing, must be taken by each one going out and when the stick was absent no one dared go out. Not infrequently confusion arose among the scholars by a race for the crooked stick; then, to restore order, the long hickory was brought down with great force on the floor, accompanied with a stamp of the foot, and a loud, husty burst of the voice. By this means order for a while was restored. Sometimes during the day my sister succeeded in getting the stick, and I started to follow her; then came the thrash, the stamp and the squall which so much frightened me that I knew not what to do--whether to go out or return to my seat--in fact I knew not what he wanted. That was the first and last day of my going to school to this pedagogue; nor was the effect for years erased from my mind, for every time I saw him (which was frequently) a similar emotion was felt, mixed however with hatred for his person.

I was about six years old before I was sent to school again. The teacher was a very different character from the former; he was clever, kind and indulgent, and the scholars loved him as a father. When I went to say my lesson he would take me upon his knees, and speak very kindly to me, and when I succeeded in saying a good lesson he never failed to praise and encourage me. The school, however, was of short duration; but during the time I learned to spell in five syllables and was exceedingly sorry when the school closed, for I loved my book and was strongly attached to my teacher.

About two years rolled away before another opportunity was offered for me to go to school. I was then entered as a scholar to a six months' school taught by a Mr. Patterson. He was also a man of easy manners, pleasant and agreeable as a teacher. But during the interim I had even forgotten my letters; consequently had to learn them a second time. But during the term, I not only learned to spell tolerably well, but also to read tolerably fluently for a boy eight years old, and at the close of the term, I acted a part of a dialogue. The teacher was popular, and at the close another six months school was made, and I was again subscribed as a scholar, and at the opening of the school I commenced writing; for in those days no one thought of putting one to writing till he could read the New Testament. Much attention was paid during this teacher's administration to spelling "by heart" as it was termed. I took much pleasure in this exercise, and sucessfully contended with the best spellers for the head of the class. I was accustomed to commit the spelling lesson to memory while going from and to school; consequently I seldom missed a word. After the second Session had been in operation about two weeks, the schoolhouse was unfortunately burnt down. And thus ended my schooldays during the time that my father lived at the old homestead on Bush Creek.

I was at quite a tender age impressed with the necessity of religion; and a lasting impression was made on my mind that I was destined ultimately to be a preacher; consequently my thoughts were not infrequently turned to this subject when perhaps not more than seven or eight years old. The first praching which I recollect of hearing was in my father's house; for the Baptist Preachers in going to their appointments at Sandy Creek, would preach at night at my father's. The name of one only is recollected, George Pope. In the meantime a new Methodist church, a log building, called Cool Spring, was built by the neighbors, and was taken into what was then known as the Deep river circuit of the South Carolina Conference. This church was about three miles from my father's. The first Methodist preacher whom I recollect hearing was Christenberry, who was in charge of the circuit, and was then called the circuit-rider. His preaching made a strong impression on my mind, and during his administration a revival of religion broke out in that church, during which my oldest brother Harden and two of my sisters Hannah and Sallie joined the church and were baptised by immersion.

Considering the character of the schools of Bush Creek, the inference would naturally follow that the people were ignorant. There were few or no educated persons in that community, and not only were they ignorant, but exceedingly superstitious. Superstition has frequently been termed the twin sister of ignorance, but I am strongly inclined to think that she is rather the daughter than the sister. There may be ignorant persons not superstitious, but the superstitious are almost invariably ignorant.

The people of this neighborhood believed in Witchcraft, Ghost-seeing, haunted houses and fortune-telling. They attributed wonderful, if not supernatural powers, to the creatures of their imaginations--witches. They believed that a witch could transform herself into any animal she chose, whether beast or bird. They also attributed to a witch the power to creep through a key-hole, by the magic of a certain bridle called the witch's bridle-- she could change any person on whom she could place it, into a horse; and then what is still more remarkable, both could come out through a key-hole, and, being mounted, she could ride this remarkable horse wherever she chose, nor would such an animal assume its identity till the bridle was removed.

From this superstitious belief in witches arose a class of imposters, called witch-doctors. They made the people believe by certain mysterious operations, that they could break the witchcraft and thus relieve these unfortunate ones from the influence of the much dreaded witch; and, in order to be sure of their pay for these machinations, they pretended they could do nothing without first being paid a certain amount of silver.

The people also believed that a witch or wizard was proof against leaden balls shot from a rifle; but could not stand before a silver bullet. They believed moreover that these witches could put spells on guns, so that the object aimed at could never be hit while such spells remained unbroken; but for all these evils they had some remedy, for they believed that there were some persons among them who possessed the peculiar art of breaking these spells.

When the neighbors came together, the most prominent topic of conversation was relating some remarkable witch tales, ghost stories and conjurations of various kinds; and so interesting was (sic) these stories that the conversation often continued till a very late hour at night. Often have I sat and listened to these stories till it seemed to me that each hair upon my head resembled the quill of a porcupine. I was afraid to go out of doors, afraid to go to bed alone, and almost afraid of my own shadow.

There were persons who professed to be fortune-tellers, and, as people are generally anxious to know their future destiny, they were willing to pay these impostors for unfolding to them the future. They could tell a young man the color of the hair, eyes, skin and many other minutiae, of the girl who was to be his wife, and describe with much exactness the kind of man that each girl would have for a husband. When it was known where one of these Fortune-tellers would operate, the house would generally be crowded throughout the day--so anxious were the people to know what neither themselves nor the fortune-teller could know. I recollect on one occasion an old, yellow man by the name of Bass, professing to be a Portuguese, called at my father's. He claimed not only to be a great fortune-teller, but he could also unfold the mystery of finding stolen or lost property; besides, he professed the peculiar power of breaking all spells and witchcraft with which persons or animals might be afflicted. The news having spread through the community, the house was filled to its utmost capacity, and the whole day was spent in fortune-telling, breaking witchcraft, and removing spells. Late in the evening, when he had disposed of most of the cases, my parents brought me up to have my fortune told. I did all I could to prevent it, but yet I was compelled to submit, and the old man took up his parable, with considerable pomp and gravity, and said, "This is no ordinary boy; he will be a ringleader, but a leader to all kinds of wickedness, such as card-playing, horse-racing and every species of gambling and finally," said he, "he will end his ignominious career on the gallows." Poor consolation to my parents and friends to know my destiny. This was a source of vexation to me as long as I remained in my father's family; for whenever I did anything mischievous or wrong, I would hear the stereotyped expression, "There, old Bass' predictions are coming true."

But after all I do not know but that I derived some benefit from these false predictions, for after several years had passed away, and I was nearly or quite grown, I was in company with several young men who were my peers, and a game of cards was proposed. I at first objected; but some one of the company argued that they only intended to play for fun or amusement, and that there was no intention of betting, consequently there could be no harm. The argument seemed reasonable and I gave up my objection. A handkerchief was spread upon the ground, and we all got around it; a pack of cards was produced, and some one of the company dealt out the cards; several cards were thrown to me with their faces downward--I picked them up and looked at them, though I did not know one card from another. But at that moment what old Bass had predicted like a flash rushed into my mind; I immediately threw the cards from my hand and peremptorily refused to play--nor could any argument induce me to play, and from that day to the present, I am not aware of having touched a card.

In the latter part of the year 1817, my father's family left the old homestead on Bush Creek, and removed some eighteen miles to the west, and settled on a plantation on what was called the Salem road, some six miles east or rather northeast of what is now Trinity college. This was an exceedingly scarce year, and those who had large families and small means, found it no easy task to procure bread enough to support their families. So scarce were provisions that the common maple was tapped, from the juice of which molasses of a very inferior quality was made; my father's family made several gallons of this kind of molasses. The following year 1818, I was sent to school some two and one half months, in the latter part of the summer and fall, to a teacher by the name of John Short, generally known as Master Short, for teachers, in those days were generally called masters. Master Short was a periodic drunkard, and though he generally bound himself in his articles to abstain from drink during his school, yet he seldom failed to violate his contract by taking sprees of drinking, which generally lasted some ten days or two weeks. His scholarship was very limited extending no farther than reading, writing and common arithmetic. In fact the higher branches, such as Grammar, Geography, Philosophy, etc., were seldom or never taught in common neighborhood schools; for I never saw an English Grammer in any school I attended. The truth is, I never saw an English Grammar to know it was one, till I was nearly twenty-six years old. In this school I learned to write, but of course very imperfectly. I very well recollect frequently writing the date 1818, being annexed to our copies. This was the last school I attended (then in my fourteenth year) during my boyhood days; but I continued to improve by applying myself to my studies at home, or where I worked.

Soon after we reacheed our new home my father and my brother Hiram erected a distillery which was a very common establishment in those days. This distillery was kept up and closely run, for the most part, night and day for some two or three years, during which time my father unfortunately acquired the habit of drinking to excess. I wish to state here, by way of parenthesis, that the last twenty-five years of his life he was a sober man and a devoted Christian, having signed a temperance pledge which he never violated.

In this connction an incident occurred which, perhaps, is worth recording. It fell to my lot to frequently aid the disdistiller especially at night, for as two stills were run, it required considerable attention and work to keep them going; consequently we were frequently aroused from an unfinished sleep, stupidity and dullness being the natural consequence, and to drive these stupid feelings away, a dram was resorted to--hence this frequent dram-drinking created a thirst for more, and, in this way I contracted a love of spirits.

On one morning having business to attend to, which required early attention, I arose at daybreak, having taken the morning dram which was as common as breakfast, I set out to attend to the business. The path led through an old field, over which a few scattering scrubby pines stood. As a clump of trees stood on the bank of the race near the path, I turned aside to say my prayers, for I was in the habit of praying morning and evening. But I could not pray; for the very attempt appeared to be sin. I arose from my knees in much confusion, and as I walked along the path, my mind was engaged in reviewing the past, trying to ascertain what could be the cause,--when an impression was made so deeply on my mind that I really thought someone spoke, and said that dram is the cause; and so fully was I under the belief that someone had spoken, that I walked around all the pines standing near, but found no one. But there and then, I resolved to abandon dram-drinking, which resolution I have adhered to through all my life, though I found it no easy matter to keep my resolution, for I had acquired an insatiable thirst for strong drinks, and as almost everybody drank around me, men, women and children, and even ministers of the gospel drank,--I found it no easy matter to resist the frequent importunities to drink. But the time, however, was not very long till the thirst subsided, and I ceased to care for it. There is danger in acquiring the habit of drinking, for it often leads to drunkenness and ruin; hence total abstinence is the only safe ground that can be occupied.

CHAPTER IV.

MY FATHER INVOLVED IN DEBT--PROPERTY SOLD--FAMILY SCATTERED.

The viper which my father had carried in his bosom for many years at length rewarded him by piercing him with its poisonous fangs. He fell under the power of strong drink which he had been long producing; he drank to excess and was frequently intoxicated, and, while in this condition, he made bad trades. He was naturally liberal-minded, but under the influence of liquor he gave with an unsparing hand--especially whiskey or brandy which was to him the same as money--and, in this way he became so deeply involved in debt that he could not pay; consequently his property was executed and sold for less than half its value. According to the laws in those days, but a very small quantity of property was exempt from execution. The family, therefore, was left in a very destitute condition.

The family at this time consisted of Father and Mother and children viz: three brothers and two Sisters. The older sister was nearly grown, but the other being the youngest of the family, was quite small. The three brothers were next to each other in the following order: William, Brantley and John Wesley. William went to live with John Bond, our brother-in-law for the purpose of learning a trade; Wesley and I were hired out. We sometimes worked at the same place, but more frequently we were separated. My Father also worked about in the nabourhood by the day, for he was not now in the habit of hunting up alcoholic liquors, but only drank too much when he came in contact with them. The two girls remained at home with mother, who was at that time in bad health.

I worked for nearly all the farmers in the neighbourhood, but more for a man by the name of John Johnson than any other, perhaps. Mr. Johnson was [a] young married man, having a wife and two small children. He was industrious and frugal, but ignorant and superstitious. He would not commence any piece of work whatever on Friday, as he regarded it as an unlucky day. He was by [no] means religious, but used profane language but seldom. Both he and his wife were very kind to me, and I loved to work for him. While I was working with Mr. Johnson an incident occurred which is perhaps worth recording. I shall merely state it as a fact, without note or comment, and leave the reader to draw his own conclusion. On a certain day we were pulling fodder. Mr. Johnson was a few paces in advance of me, when he suddenly stopped, and turning round, looked me steadily in the face, and said without even a smile, "Brantley, you will make a preacher, and when you become a preacher, I want you to tell me what to do." That man lived to hear me preach two or three sermons, and in a short time after he was taken sick, and died.

On one occasion my brother Wesley and I were sent to work for a man who lived some eight or nine miles from our home. It was in the month of November and when we left home the weather was pleasant. We had shoes, but no socks or coats. Soon after we reached the place of our destination, the weather turned quite cold and very heavy frosts fell at night. We with the negroes were sent out before sunrise to pull corn. The corn was on the low-grounds of a creek, where the cuckleburrs and spanish needles were as high or higher than our heads. We suffered extremely from the cold. This was our lot every morning. Our fare also was bad, especially supper. The man for whom we worked possessed no small amount of property. He was a little past middle age, but his wife (as she was the second) was very young. She was the mother of one child only--that was an infant; but there were five or six other children whose mother was dead. None of them were grown. Though our fare was bad, we fared just as his own children. I never saw him at the table when we ate. His wife however generally waited on the table. We were told by some of the work hands that he and his wife ate at a different table and had very different fare. This however I did not see. He was a local preacher in the M. E. Church, though his walk was by no means exemplary; for we never heard him pray, nor did either he or his wife ever spend any time with the family after supper. We worked with him some four or five days, and on either Thursday or Friday in the afternoon we were sent into the orchard to gather apples. One string of the fence enclosing the orchard was hard by the road leading homeward. We watched our opportunity, and when we thought no one saw us, we climbed over the fence and took the road for home; nor did we travel slowly, for we ran a large fraction of the way and reached home about dark.

This was the only time that I ever ran away from the place where I worked, and had a good reason for doing it this time, for our work was very hard and our fare very bad. Early next morning this man came to take us back, but we peremptorily refused to go; nor did father try to make us. How little did that man think that the poor boy whom he treated so badly would be the educator of his children, for four of them were afterwards in the school where I was Principal.

CHAPTER V.

REMOVAL OF THE FAMILY.

In the latter part of the year 1820 (as I now recollect) the family removed westward some five miles, and occupied a house belonging to William Leach Esq., located in the immediate neighborhood in which Trinity College now stands. While here I worked for nearly all the farmers in the neighborhood of Trinity College, but more for Mr. Leach than any other man. Early in the spring of 1821, while with several others in piling logs in a new-ground, as six of us were carrying a log with hand spikes, I and a boy about my size were at the butt end, I having hold of the sharpened end of the handspike. The two that were carrying at the smaller end let their end of the log fall, jerking the handspike out of my hands, as I was making a step with my right foot; the end of the handspike struck me on the instep with great force, making a deep cut. For several minutes my leg was paralyzed to the knee, having no sensation in it at all, and had I judged from the sense of feeling only, my conclusion would have been, that my leg was off at the knee. I was not able to walk for some two months. As soon as I was able to work, I went to work for a gentleman by the name of Josiah Blair, who sent me to plough in a field nearly a quarter of a mile from the house, directing me when I heard the trumpet to come to breakfast and bring the horse with me. Accordingly I turned out and started to the house. As I was crossing a branch of the Uwharrie the horse stopped to drink and while he was drinking, I got down on a large rock that was not covered by water, with a view of washing my hands and face, and while I was washing the horse stepped upon my naked foot, and it on the rock. It was the same foot that was hurt by the handspike. It was literally crushed. How I reached the bank I never knew, and I was for some time nearly or quite unconscious. I was aroused from this swooning state by someone shaking me. I was taken home, nor was I able to work any more for about four months. Soon after I began to walk on my foot it commenced hurting me, the first sensation being that of a fine brier or nettle deeply seated in the ball of my foot. Frequent efforts were made to extract it but none could be found. I left home on Monday morning as I now recollect to work during the week for a man living some five or six miles distant. I continued working till Friday evening though in much pain. I then left for home intending to remain there till my foot became well, but on Saturday morning Mr. Leach sent for me to come and help his hands pull fodder. I put an old shoe on my foot and went, and when I returned at night my foot was worse, but next morning being Sunday, it was said "a big meeting" was going on some six miles distant, and as several young people of both sexes were going afoot, I also determined to go, and pressed my foot, though considerably swollen into my shoe and walk(ed) to the church. At the close of the exercise, it was announced that during the evening a meeting would be held at a private house. Though it was a mile and a half or two miles out of the way, my company resolved to go, though none of us had had any dinner. During the exercises the pain in my foot was excrutiating, and at the close of the meeting, I found myself unable to walk a step. The question now was "how am I to get home." But as there were two boys in the company both taller than myself, I placed a hand on a shoulder of each, and hopped home a distance of four miles. It is impossible for me to give anyone an adequate idea of the intensity of my suffering for the next two or three weeks; so during the year '21 I suffered much and worked but little.

While working for Mr. Leach I found a warm sympathizer and fast friend in the person of Mrs. Leach. She was a lady, though not thoroughly educated, of a strong mind and fluent in conversation. One day at the dinner table she said to me in her familiar way, "Brantley, your hair is too long for this hot weather, wouldn't you like to have it trimmed?" I answered in the affirmative. "Well," said she, "when dinner is over come into my room, and I will trim it for you." After trimming my hair she placed the palm of her hand against my forehead, with her fingers extending up into my hair, pressed my head up erect, and stepping back she looked me straight in the face and remarked, "Brantley, you will not always be in the field working with negroes." These words fell upon my ear as words of prophecy, for though I had an insatiable thirst for an education, I had not as yet seen how it was to be obtained, for I had neither time nor books to study; but that lady lived to see her prediction fulfilled, for she often heard me preach and lecture, and saw me the principal of a high school.

While we lived on Mr. Leach's place I frequently worked for a class of people call(ed) Quakers, or Friends. These were generally well-to-do farmers, and as they were religiously opposed to slavery, they hired frequently, and generally speaking they were a clever, sober, industrious people, and always treated me kindly.

I frequently worked for an elderly man by the name of Enos Blair, and on one occasion, while I was working for him, the Quarterly Meeting to be held at Marlboro Church was near. I heard them speak of a watermelon patch in the garden, but the old gentleman refused to let any be pulled, as he was keeping them for the accommodation of his friends whom he expected to visit him during the meeting. One day while in company with two of my comrades, both of whom were older and larger than myself--in fact they were nearly or quite grown--I happened to speak of this watermelon patch, with no specified intention as I recollect. They immediately proposed to go and steal them, and thus disappoint "the old Quakers," as they called them. I objected, as the very thought of stealing was revolting to my mind; but they argued the case, and said we had just as much right to the melons as the "old Quakers" as they neither belonged to us nor to them. Fallacious as this argument was, it had the desired effect upon my mind. I yielded and consented to go with them. The night before the meeting commenced was fixed upon as the proper time to commit the deed. Accordingly we met. One of them having a sack. We proceeded to the scene of action and when we reached the place, the plan of operation was agreed upon. It fell to my lot to stand between the house and garden, to watch as a sentinel. One of the others was to go into the garden and pull the melons, and hand them over the garden palings to the other, who put them into the sack as he received them. Every melon was pulled that could be found, but it was no pleasant thing for me, for before the thing was accomplished, I deeply regretted that I had engaged in it, but the deed was done, and no one knew it. A pole was procured and the sack of melons placed on it. We then moved stealthily away. On reaching a persimmon tree which stood in the old field we stopped, and ate as many of the melons as we could. By this time a very angry looking cloud had arisen in the West and proclaimed its approach by deep-toned thunder. We gathered up our stolen property and set out for home. The weather was very warm, and seed ticks abundant, and as we tredged along we gathered our full share. The cloud rapidly advanced--the lightning was almost constantly flashing and the thunder becoming louder and louder. We were compelled to take shelter in a barn which was well filled with bearded wheat. We crawled up on the wheat near the roof. It was a fearful storm. The thunder was terrific. The lightning was almost constantly glaring and the rain fell in torrents. Never can I forget that night. It was the most wretched of my life. The ticks, the heat, and the bearded wheat were all instruments of torture, but far worse than all the rest combined, were the goadings of the guilty conscience. I was horribly damned, for I felt as if I could not live till morning. At length daylight appeared, and we hastened to get away, but one proposed however that before leaving we should take another mess of watermelons. This however I refused, having no taste for stolen melons. I hastened home; but my guilty conscience went with me. A few days after I went back to work for the same old man. While at the breakfast table a small boy, a grandson of the old gentleman, said to me, "Brantley, some mean rascals came here and stole all of grandfather's melons." My feelings at that time I have no language to describe. If I looked as guilty as I felt, it is a wonder they did not know I was one. This was the first and the last time that I ever engaged in stealing melons or anything else. If Franklin paid too dear for his whistle, I paid too dear for the watermelons.

CHAPTER VI.

THE MORAL CONDITIONS OF THE NEIGHBORHOOD--A YOUNG LADY CONVERTED AT A DANCE FROLIC--A REVIVAL OF RELIGION.

I have never known any community or neighborhood more completely demoralized than was this. Very few of the heads of the families made any pretensions to religion or morality and the light of those that did, appeared to be under a bushel; for I never heard a blessing asked at the table or a prayer offered in any family, either by night or morning. Preaching was seldom--prayer-meetings never nor was there any such thing as Sunday-school. Sabbaths were desecrated, for the young people would frequently assemble together on Sunday, to play at cards or engage in some game of diversion. Books were circulated among them which were of the most vulgar and demoralizing character, and eagerly read, espeecially by the young men and large boys. Though a preacher lived in the neighborhood, and also an exhorter, however religious they may have been personally, they, like Eli of old, utterly failed to restrain their children. Few and feeble were the checks to the downward course of the youth of both sexes. The Athenians in the days of St. Paul were not perhaps more fully devoted to the worship of idols, than were the young people of this neighborhood to the worship of the god of pleasure; for they held weekly two dance frolics on Wednesday and Saturday nights, and as all came who chose without regard to character or morality, it may be safely inferred that these frolics were very disorderly and demoralizing. But a change came, and the cause of that change was not a little remarkable. Some minister preached on Sunday previous to the wednesday night dance, and Miss Ester Morgan who was an expert in dancing was convicted. But she concealed her state of mind even from her father who was a member of the church and also an Exhorter. The Wednesday night dance came on, when several young men called at Mr. Morgan's to gallant the girls to the frolic. Miss Ester however manifested an unwillingness to go; but being importuned and pressed, she consented and went.

The party having assembled, and ready to commence, the young men began to select their partners, but Miss Ester refused to dance with any. This doubtless was surprising to all; but when they commenced their exercise and the music began, she dropped upon her knees and began praying aloud. This was to the party as a clap of thunder in a clear sky, and perhaps if an earthquake had shaken the house, the alarm would not have been greater, for a greater part of them left the house and fled as for life. The fiddler fled for home and some two or three with him, and one that was with him made the following statement to me: "We went over fences and through corn fields, taking the nearest way for home, and as I heard the blades of corn cracking behind me, I felt certain that the Devil was right after me, and on reaching the door of the house we didn't waited (sic) for any one to open, but broke down the door and jumped into bed and covered up head and ears without pulling shoes, hat, coat, or a rag (of) clothes off, and were almost afraid to breathe, lest the Devil should hear us in our concealment." Only a few had courage enough to stand their ground. These sent for the young lady's father and some other members of the church and so the dance frolic was turned into a prayer-meeting, and just before day the young lady was converted.

So dance frolics ended and prayer-meetings began. A revival of religion spread all over that community, and nearly all the young people of both sexes professed religion and joined the church.

Religion flourished and schools revived, for they generally go hand in hand. This neighborhood (the neighborhood of Trinity College) has for more than a half century been distinguished for religion, morality and learning.

CHAPTER VII.

THE FAMILY REMOVES--ENGAGES IN FARMING--FIRST CAMP-MEETING--CONVICTION AND CONVERSION.

In the spring of '22, we rented a plantation on Muddy Creek, then called the Lowe Place. Since then it was occupied by Mr. William Robins, now deceased. The place is about two and one-half miles East of Trinity College, and about one and one-half or two miles from the Leach Place which we left. The land was tolerably fertile, and paid the cultivater (sic) well. There was also a good orchard both of apple and peach trees. We were successful in farming, and raised plenty of all kinds of grain. Nothing of particular interest occurred during this year. In the early part of August, '23, a camp-meeting was held at Ebenezer Church--the first of the kind that I had ever seen. The wooden tents were made of poles and all slatted one way. The doors were very low, insomuch that it looked very much like crawling into a tent, also some families occupied cloth tents. The only covering about the arbor was over the altar. Lewis Skidmore was the Presiding Elder, and Joachim Lowe was the preacher in charge. Other preachers were in attendance whose names I do not recollect, though there were three Local preachers living in the neighborhood, viz.: James Needham, Alson Gray and Joseph Clark. These were active workers in the altar. Skidmore was a man something above the mediumsize--his voice clear, loud and impressive. The people seemed to think he was the greatest man in the world and every effort was made by both men and women to go out and hear the Elder, and indeed he was worth hearing. The meeting resulted in great success; many professed religion and were added to the church. Though I had been from early boyhood religiously impressed, my convictions had passed off and I had become rather careless and indifferent, and was really afraid of the preachers. My brother-in-law James Coltrane was tented there, and some of the preachers were there almost at every meal. If I knew they were there, I would not go though my sister urged me strongly. So she would watch her opportunity and bring me something to eat wherever she could find me. I went to the meeting on Saturday, and continued there till Tuesday afternoon. I then went home with the intention not to return. I [had] listened to the preaching generally and attentively; but it had but a slight effect upon my mind. Soon after I reached home Tuesday evening, three or four of my comrades came along going to the meeting. They called to me and asked if I were not going. I told them I was not; for I believed I had got about enough of the camp-meeting; but they insisted and I went with them. We were engaged in laughing and talking and cracking jokes on the way to the meeting; but when we got within about half a mile of the camp-ground, we heard the shouting and singing of the people--conviction immediately seized upon my mind. I had no more taste for merriment of any kind, and to avoid hearing my comrades laugh and talk I fell behind, and on reaching the campground I saw several of my friends male and female who were as I thought as wicked as myself when I left, now apparently as happy as Seraphs. This deepened my convictions and I became exceedingly anxious to feel what I believed they felt.

Soon after reaching the campground the sun set--night drew on, the camp ground was illuminated, the trumpet sounded and the people eagerly gathered around the stand to hear what the Lord would speak. I had not as yet decided to go into the altar, but thought it more than probable that I would after hearing the sermon; consequently I occupied a seat not far from the altar door. The sermon was listened to with marked attention, and at its close there was quite a stir among the people--many were pressing into the altar; others were weeping, who did not go. My friend Mr. Ahi Robins, who sat near me, cried out aloud, "Help me to get into the altar, and keep the Devil from cheating me out of my soul." I was strongly urged by many to go into the altar, but I would not go, notwithstanding the load of sin was heavy. I left the congregation and sought some secret place for prayer and meditation. Not a few difficulties were presented to my mind by the Tempter, I suppose; such as: "the time was when you might have obtained religion, but it is now too late--you are a reprobate, and it is useless to try, and, if you are not, you are young and there is plenty of time yet to attend to this work." A thunder cloud was now perceived to be approaching, rumbling thunder augmented the solemnity of the scene, and when it was perceived that the cloud would come over, all the penitents that were outside the altar (for the altar could not contain all) were taken to the church. I also went into the church, and took a seat. Notwithstanding there was singing, shouting, praying, and talking, I paid but little attention to it, for I was trying to come to a decision, which at length I did. I decided to seek religion there, and then. I set no limit to the time I would seek, only the close of life. As soon as I had reached the conclusion, I knelt at my seat without being invited to do so by anyone. I commenced praying as earnestly as I knew how. At length I found myself lying on the floor with my head in someone's lap; but when or how I got into that position, I know not. For some time I was perplexed with the harassing thought that my wicked comrades were laughing at me. The burden was heavy and the struggle long. My friends were constantly bringing news to me that this one and that one had obtained religion, and among them was my friend Mr. Ahi Robins. Finally they told me that every penitent had obtained religion but myself--not, perhaps, less than fifty in number. The night was now far spent and day was approaching. At length, however, I reached a state of mind that I cared not who laughed nor who cried. I had now become willing to be anything--to do anything--or to suffer anything in order to be relieved of the burden which seemed intolerable to be borne. It was suggested to my mind in the form of a question, "What hinders since you have given all up." At that moment the burden left, and I felt perfectly easy; but knew not what had removed it. I could not say that I had religion, for that I did not know; but my faith had wonderfully increased; and I fully believed if I asked to know, the petition would be answered, and scarcely was the petition formed in my mind when I was filled unutterably full of glory and of God.

How I arose from my position I know not nor ever did. The first thing of which I have any distinct recollection as attracting my attention was that a Local preacher by the name of Joseph Clark was holding me in his arms, and singing:

> I little thought He'd been so nigh,
> His speaking makes me laugh and cry.

After the ecstasy had somewhat subsided, and I had become cool enough to think, I really thought I had lost all my weight, and, in order to convince myself of the fact, I went out of doors and walked upon the leaves in order to ascertain whether they would give way under my feet or not; but I found I was mistaken. As well as I recollect, day was now just beginning to break. It was the 12th day of August, 1823. At eight o'clock the trumpet sounded and the people for the last time during that meeting gathered around the stand. The door was open to receive members, and I without consulting father or mother, brother or sister or anyone else, went into the altar, and gave my hand to the preacher in charge, and from that day to this (1886) I have been a member of the M. E. or the M. E. Church, South.

CHAPTER VIII.

SECRET PRAYER--CLASS MEETINGS--BAND MEETINGS.

After the eight o'clock service at which time the camp-meeting broke, as stated in the previous chapter, I set out for home; but as my ecstasy of joy had subsided, the tempter as sailed me, urging that I had lost my religion, and that it was impossible for anyone to keep it any length of time; consequently the only possible way to ever reach heaven would be to get religion just before death. This temptation rendered me miserable, for I did not know that it proceeded from the tempter. On reaching home I scarcely knew what to say. I could say I knew I had religion at the camp-meeting, but I could not say that I had it then. I was anxious for night to come on that I might resort to secret prayer, and when the evening shades prevailed I sought the most secret place that I could for prayer. I went nearly a quarter of a mile from the house to a papaw thicket and there I wrestled, Jacob-like, until I obtained a blessing, and made the happy discovery that I had not lost my religion. I returned to the house rejoicing. I think I learned from experience that secret prayer is essential to the maintenance of a religious principle and feeling in the heart. Both preachers and class leaders insisted most strenuously on the observance of secret prayer as an indispensable duty, and this to be efficient, must be habitual.

Class meetings in those days were held as regularly as preaching, and indeed more frequently; for every leader held a meeting at least once or twice between the times of preaching, and the preacher in charge scarcely ever failed to hold a class meeting immediately after preaching.

These class meetings were generally very useful and edifying; but some leaders held their class meetings in such a way that they were scarcely either edifying or profitable. The leader would generally select some member to assist him, and while the members kept up continual singing would go around and talk to each member on his seat; consequently the members generally could hear scarcely nothing of what the leader or members said; but other leaders adopted a different method. The leader would stand and call the name of each member, when the name was called the member would rise, and the leader would examine him as to his present enjoyments in religion, whether he was regular in the discharge of his secret prayer and whether he enjoyed religion in the home circle. He would then give such advice as the nature of the case demanded. This method was highly edifying and profitable. The leader would also occasionally sing a stanza or two of a hymn adapted to the state of mind of certain members, the other members also joining with him in singing. This tended to make the meeting intensely interesting as well as instructive.

After the camp-meeting held at the same place, Ebenezer Church, in '24, the class became so large that it was found expedient to divide it into three sections, a leader being appointed to each section. One of these leaders held a meeting each Sunday, except on the regular preaching day. Any member of the class had a right to attend every meeting; but the leader examined none except the members of his own section.

Rev. Alson Gray was my first class leader, who subsequently acquired some notoriety as a preacher in the M. P. Church. Franklin Harris was my next leader. He was a man of piety and good sense, and of agreeable manners. Ahi Robins was my next and last leader at Ebenezer; he was a man of strong feeling and deep piety, and was highly esteemed by the members of his class. The two former have gone to their reward, but Brother Robins is still living (18-86). It was a rare thing in those days for one to backslide; for the young converts were tenderly nursed and watched over by their leaders. The General Conference which removed the obligation of members to attend class meeting may have rendered the church more popular, but I think less vitally pious.

In those days the Methodist discipline provided for the formation of Band Meetings. These bands were rather peculiar, for not only males and females met separately, but also married and unmarried persons met separately. In consequence of this peculiarity it was impracticable for women in the country to meet in Band Societies; hence the rule could only be carried out so far as women were concerned, in towns and cities. In the neighborhood in which I resided, both the married and unmarried men formed bands which met at different places. There were only five young men who belonged to the young mens' band. viz.: John Gray, William Gray, Ahi Robins, William Lenard and myself. We met weekly at night, in an old schoolhouse, and, according to the rules of the band, each one in turn acted as leader. Each meeting was opened by reading the scriptures, singing a hymn, and prayer by the leader, after which the leader made a statement of his religious experience during the past week involving such as temptation, trial, religious enjoyment, etc. Each member was then called upon to make a similar statement of his experience,--never going back beyond the week. The meeting was then closed by singing another hymn, and prayer by some one of the members.

    I found the exercises of these meetings to be very advantageous to me, though at first it was very embarrassing to act as leader; for I was naturally timid and retiring in my manners. The band continued to meet about twelve months and would doubtless have continued longer, but for the dispersion of several of the members. But this was long enough to endear the members to ach other.

CHAPTER IX.

1824-1837--CAMP MEETINGS--THE MINISTRY--TEACHING.

At this time ('24, '25, '26) camp meetings were held in various places in different counties and were generally attended with the happiest results. It was nothing uncommon for one hundred converts to be the result of a single meeting. In the latter part of August, 1824, a camp meeting was held in the southern portion of Randolph County at a church called Salem. I and two other young men resolved to go--previous to that time we had never been to a camp meeting, except at Ebenezer. Having prepared biscuits for our journey (for we expected to board ourselves, and sleep in the altar, as the weather was warm) we set out early on Saturday morning for the camp meeting and reached the camp ground about the time the tent holders were at dinner. We were agreeably surprised on being invited to dinner, for we expected no such hospitality. Our next care was to have our horses provided for. This having been done, we felt quite satisfied, though all were strangers except two preachers. Christopher Thomas was the preacher in charge--he was a good preacher and a most devoted Christian. A few years after he was stationed in the town of Newberne, and after having the most extensive revival of religion ever known in that place, he died a most triumphant death.

When night came on we were kindly provided for in the way of sleeping. Some thirty or thirty-five tents were occupied--much larger and of a better quality than those at Ebenezer. The people were unusually kind, the preaching was good and we enjoyed ourselves finely--so much so that I would have been glad if it had lasted a month. There was a considerable revival; there were many penitents in the altar and not a few converts. Here for the first time I began to work in the altar. The meeting closed on the Wednesday morning following and we parted with those kind friends with many tears. We then set out for home, feeling and believing that camp meetings were the next door to Paradise.

On reaching home we heard that a camp meeting was to be held in Guilford County, at a church called Pleasant Garden, commencing on the following Friday night. We resolved to go, but did not get ready to start till after dinner on Saturday. We then set out, full of the spirit of camp meetings, expecting a rich feast of enjoyment; but night overtook us before we reached the camp ground and we thought it best to stop and wait till morning. We were kindly entertained by the family with whom we lodged; but we were so eager for the camp meeting we refused to remain for breakfast, believing that we should be amply supplied when we reached the camp ground. In this, however, we were a little mistaken. When we reached the camp ground the people were generally engaged at their breakfast. Our first care was to secure a place for our horses. This was soon done, for we obtained a good pasture for them near the camp ground, but we missed our breakfast. But this we regarded as a mere accident, having arrived at an unpropitious time. We cared, however, but little for this; for we would only be the better prepared for dinner, as we thought of course that we would be fully known by dinner, for we were sure that three strangers of some distinction would attract attention. It never once occurred to our minds that it was necessary for us to introduce ourselves or to apply to the P. C.,

* P. C., means Preacher of Circuit. [Ed.]

for a home; but to our astonishment and chagrin dinner came on and they had not found us out yet, nor had we any biscuits as at the other camp meeting to resort to, feeling well assured that we would be well supplied as we had been at the other meeting. But alas! supper came on, and we were still unknown. By this time we began to feel a little slim--we had stood about and walked about and yet no one had noticed us. We now began to think that something would have to be done, but what to do we knew not, for we had no money, and to beg we were ashamed. Night came on--the trumpet sounded and the people gathered about the stand to hear preaching. We were there (for we never missed a sermon) but soon after taking my seat, I was taken quite sick. After preaching was over I lay down upon a bench. There was a gentleman standing near me. I asked him if he knew where I could obtain a place to lie down as I was quite sick. He said he did not, but would try to find one. He left, but soon returned, informing me that he had secured a place for me to sleep. He conducted me to it (it was the sitting part of a tent), with a wagon sheet spread upon straw. This was rather poor accommodation for a sick man, but I was glad to get it. I lay down upon this sheet without undressing, and after some time I fell asleep, and, when I awoke, it was day and the family was stirring. I remained till breakfast but received no invitation to eat. We now got together and concluded that we had better try to get home while we had sufficient strength to do it, and, as I was unwell, my two friends proposed to go for the horses. While they were gone I took a walk, and as I walked I met a company of persons coming from the neighborhood of Trinity College, and among them was my friend Mrs. William Leach. She saluted me in her familiar way, "Well, Brantley, how are you getting along?"

"Not very well," was my answer.

"Why, what is the matter? Don't they feed you?"

"I have eaten nothing since Saturday night."

"Well, well, that is a hard case; come along with me, I have brought a lunch for myself, but you've got to eat it."

I gladly accepted the offer. About the time I finished eating, my friends came with the horses. We mounted and left for home. This was Monday morning about eleven o'clock, having eaten nothing since Saturday night. We wondered how people in adjoining counties could be so different.

Some fifteen years after this occurrence, I was invited to attend a camp meeting held at this same place; but things had very much changed. Then I was a youth without education and green enough--now I was a preacher and Principal of a high school. I preached each day of the meeting, nor did I lack for anything to eat; but I scarcely ever looked over the congregation without thinking of our starving time at that place.

Perhaps the starving time through which I passed at this camp meeting, though a bitter pill to me, resulted in some good; for in after years, in attending camp meeting as a preacher, I made it my business to look out for green boys, as I was once, and have arrangements made for their accommodations, for I have never forgotten what I passed through at the first camp meeting I ever attended at Pleasant Garden. Wealth and position are scarcely ever overlooked; but those on the lower rounds of society are frequently neglected, and it is sometimes the case that the neglected ones make the most distinguished and useful men.

Some ten years having rolled away after I attended camp meeting at Salem, I returned to that place as a preacher, and when I arose to preach to the people the first time, on looking over the congregation and recognizing the faces of many friends who had treated me so kindly when a mere youth, my emotions may be imagined but never described. Nor was my preaching, imperfect as it was, without an effect upon the congregation.

Camp meetings recently have lost much of their power and usefulness, and as every effect must have a cause, there is a cause or causes for this decline, nor does it require a very close observer to perceive some of the causes at least, which have produced this deplorable effect. Members of the church do not seem to feel as deep interest as formerly, and are not so willing to make the necessary preparation; and as these meetings have lost their novelty, the attendance is generally quite thin till Sunday, and this being a kind of show day, but little good is generally accomplished, and as the tent holders are few in numbers, and consequently are pressed with the number they have to entertain, in consequence of this they generally break up as early as Tuesday or Wednesday morning succeeding the Sabbath. The only apparent remedy for these failures is to have fewer of them and to continue them some ten or twelve days.

During the year '24 a library Society was formed at Ebenezer Church, at which place I held my membership. The society was regularly organized and officered. The payment of $2.00 and an annual tax of twenty-five cents was the condition of membership. The society met quarterly and at each meeting the books were all brought together and the names of the members written on a slip of paper, and put into a hat, and as they were drawn out each member took choice of the books that were on hand, but if one was disposed to pay four or six dollars, he drew a book for each share. I put in first only one share, but that did not satisfy me. I continued to put in till I had four shares, and though engaged in working on a farm, read about one thousand pages a week. The society flourished for some three years, during which time I read a large number of books. But my thirst for knowledge led me to read too much, more than I could assimilate. But notwithstanding this, the library was no small source of improvement to myself and others, and any similar institution cannot fail to be a blessing to any community.

When about twenty years old I hired to a gentleman by the name of Robbins, as a distiller. His establishment was large, and required the constant attention of two distillers. At first I was only an assistant, but soon after I entered the establishment the principal distiller left, and I was employed as the principal distiller. But I saw so much wickedness caused by drinking that I was led to doubt the morality of the business, and after reflecting on it for some weeks, I became thoroughly convinced that it was wrong. Consequently, I determined to abandon it, notwithstanding I was making much higher wages than I could possibly make on the farm, and though my employer was exceedingly unwilling to give me up,--yet I abandoned the business forever.

In the year '26, when I was about twenty-one years old, I and another young man by the name of Emsly Leach rented ground from Lewis Leach, Esq., and raised a crop of corn and cotton.

Though I was impressed at a very tender age that I must preach, yet for several years after my conversion, I was not impressed that I was called to preach. But while engaged in cultivating this crop, the impression returned with great force, so much so that I could scarcely sleep at night. The impression pursued me wherever I went, nor could I find any permanent peace, till I solemnly promised the good Lord that as soon as I could make preparation I would undertake it. In the meantime I went to a gold mine to work, and not long after engaging in the gold mining, I was employed to do the business for a large portion of the mine, and for sometime I made money very fast. The temptation was then presented to me, to which I unfortunately yielded, to put off preaching till I acquired considerable means, and then I would have no difficulty in entering upon the work, but in the course of less than eighteen months, instead of getting rich I lost all I had made, and was compelled to struggle with debt, and I could see no opening for me to preach. But at length, I determined to make the effort and quit my mining and manual labor of every kind. In December, 1831, I commenced teaching school at Bethlehem Church, Guilford County, North Carolina. In a few weeks after, I was appointed class leader by the P. C. I had previously held my membership at Pleasant Garden for several years, and when application was made for license to exhort, it was made to the society at P. G., but that society refused to grant them, being influenced by a Local preacher and a class leader, who said they didn't believe that I could ever make a preacher,--but I thought I knew my duty and resolved to do it. My membership being removed to Bethlehem, no further opposition was offered.

I here record, by way of parenthesis, my first marriage. On the 31st of January, 1828, I was united in holy matrimony, by Rev. John Coe, to Miss Fannie Sherwood, daughter of Daniel and Rachel Sherwood, of Guilford County, N. C. At the time of my marriage I was twenty-three years and twenty-seven days old, and my wife nearly nineteen. We lived pleasantly together for nearly six years; then death severed the union, and she now lies beside her infant son in the graveyard of Pleasant Garden Church.

I now had license to exhort, but to begin was a heavy cross. I preached my first sermon in my brother Hardin's house in Randolph County, from Romans 6th chapter and 23rd verse. This sermon was preached before I had license at all. At the opening of the spring of '32 I commenced preaching at Bethlehem Church once in two weeks, and also on Sunday evening at the widow Field's. I also established a Sabbath school at Bethlehem, which was largely attended. In a few weeks a revival broke out which continued some two or three months, during which time there were many converts and considerable accessions were made to the church. I continued teaching at Bethlehem for nearly two years. In the fall of '33 I was licensed to preach. The P. E. who signed my license was the sainted John W. Childs.

* P. E., abbreviation for Presiding Elder. [Ed,]

Late in the fall of '32, before I was licensed to preach, I was invited to Cool Spring Church and York's school-house, in Randolph County. The appointment stood at the schoolhouse on Saturday night and at the church on Sunday. There was a good effect at the schoolhouse, as there were some four or five penitents. On Sunday there was a signal display of divine power. The whole church was an altar, there were several converts, but the number is now forgotten. This revival was extensive, as it extended to all the adjacent neighborhoods, and lasted for several months. I continued preaching through the winter on Saturday night and Sunday at Cool Spring, and very many were added to different churches. Revival also broke out at Wood's schoolhouse, where (I) preached on Sunday nights, where no society had been formed. In this work I was aided by Brother William Anderson, the P. C. From the fruits of this revival a society was formed, and a new church erected called Randolph Church.

In the latter part of the summer of 1833, I left Bethlehem and taught a three month school near Pleasant Garden Church. In a few days after I was licensed to preach, I attended a camp meeting at a place called Troy's Camp-ground. At this camp meeting I preached several times. The meeting was quite successful, and not long after a church was erected, named Bethel, which I believe is still in a flourishing condition.

In the last of October or first part of November, I left the neighborhood of Pleasant Garden and took charge of a school on Sandy Creek in Randolph County in a thickly settled neighborhood, generally called Ellison Town. I continued fifteen months, during which time I preached at various private houses in the neighborhood, insomuch that one man remarked that I had preached at every man's house, except his "ash-hopper." I also preached regularly at the school-house, in which I taught; nor was the preaching in vain, for we had a considerable revival at the school house. While teaching this school, I lost my affectionate wife, who died on the 14th day of January, 1834, leaving one living child. But my loss was doubtless her eternal gain for her death was most triumphant. She remarked to me a little before she died, "I have no desire to live but for you and little Rachel."

While engaged in teaching this school in June, '34, I held my first two days meeting at Troy's Academy, though as has already been stated, I had the clearest possible evidence of my call to the ministry, yet I was frequently assailed by the tempter, urging that this was only a notion of mine--that there was no such thing as a real call to the ministry. I was very much concerned about this two days meeting, and as it was to be held on the very eve of harvest, I was harrassed with the thought that there would be but very few in attendance. Some night or two before the meeting was to commence, I had a very remarkable dream, which forever settled the question in my mind as to the genuineness of my call to the ministry. I was boarding at this time with a Mr. Thos. Ellison. The family was devotedly pious.

THE DREAM.

I dreamed that a large flock of partridges was before me, and around my feet was a large number of white stones or pebbles about the size of a partridge egg, though perfectly round and transparent; and I gathered my hands full of these pebbles and threw them among the partridges, and as I now recollect, thirteen was the number killed. The success excited me and I awoke, and I spent several minutes in reflecting on the dream. It seemed a little remarkable to me, as I was no sportsman, but closely engaged in studying; but as soon as possible, I dismissed it as a dream merely, and fell asleep, and dreamed again that the partridges represented the people that would be at the two days meeting--that the white stones represented the words that would be preached, and that the number killed represented the number of people that would be saved at this meeting. Again I awoke and found myself not a little excited, and after reflecting for some time on this dream and interpretation, I again fell asleep and the dream and the interpretation were both repeated, which made a deep impression on my mind. The morning came, and as there were several boarders in the school [who] wished to go, and as conveyances were almost impossible, we set out early afoot, though the distance was ten miles,--but my mind was so deeply impressed that I could not enjoy the company. I had not, as yet, told the dream to anyone. There was a young man in the company who was studying for the ministry. I concluded to tell the dream to him, as it might somewhat relieve the burden that pressed so heavily on my mind. We fell a little behind the others and I related my dream to him. He appeared to be full of faith and said, "As certain as there is a God in heaven, the dream will come to pass." I requested him to keep it a secret until the meeting should have passed. On arriving at the place, I found a larger number of people in attendance than I had expected. I preached from the text: "O Lord revive thy work," and when penitents were invited, some five or six presented themselves at the altar, and after singing and praying for some time, the congregation was dismissed, and an appointment made for the night.

When the hour had arrived we met according to appointment, and the congregation had very much increased in number, and after preaching, the penitents were again invited, when some ten or twelve presented themselves at the altar, but no one professed. The following day a love-feast meeting was held at nine o'clock a. m, and preaching at eleven. The love-feast meeting was well attended, and the members of the church appeared to enjoy themselvs well, and when penitents were invited quite a number presented themselves. When eleven o'clock had arrived, the congregation was so large that we were compelled to go to the grove, and I preached from the text, "Escape for thy life." The effect was powerful, and a large number presented themselves at the altar for prayer, and not a few of these were wealthy and influential, but only one made a profession of religion. This now appeared to be the time for breaking up the meeting, and while I was considering what course to adopt, brother Troy approached me and said: "Brother York, this meeting must not be broken up." But I said, "What can I do. The school is to commence tomorrow morning, and the distance as you know is ten miles." He replied, "Appoint meeting for this afternoon, and I will see to your getting to the school." This was done, and a large congregation was in attendance before the hour arrived. I preached again, and the effect again was very powerful, and many presented themselves at the altar at prayer. We continued working with the penitents till dark, and while they were lighting up the room, one of the most remarkable events occurred in the history of my life, for almost as sudden as a flash of lightning, every penitent was converted, and such a time I have scarcely ever witnessed. And after the excitemnt had a little subsided, at the request of Brother Troy, I opened the door to receive members, when thirteen gave me their hands and their names, and thus, as it appears to me, my dream was literally fulfilled.

At the close of my school here I went to Salem Church near Franklinville, Randolph County, and taught there twelve months. During my teaching there and at Ellison town we formed a temperance society in Salem Church which was very prosperous for several years, and no doubt accomplished much good. I frequently preached and lectured on Temperance at various places in the surrounding country, and formed societies at different places. In the summer of '35, I was elected president of Randolph Temperance Society, the meetings of which were held at each court at Asheboro.

When this school closed I went to York's schoolhouse, at which place a subscription school had been raised for nine months. While here I commenced lecturing on Nat. Phy. on Saturday evenings. For the benefit [of the students] I also formed a night class and instructed the students in Grammar and Arithmetic. And while here I married the second time--to Miss Mary Wells Lineberry. We were united in marriage on November 13th, 1836. In the community of this schoolhouse I preached and lectured frequently on temperance. I formed a society in the town of New Salem, which continued in successful operation for several years. After the school had closed here, a school was made in a new school-house near Walker's Mills, same county, named Piney Grove, in the immediate neighborhood of Old Union Meeting-house, as it used to be called, at which place the first camp-meeting was ever held in Randolph County.

A short time before this meeting commenced, one of Mr. Bell's negro women dreamed that she went from that camp meeting (to be held soon) to heaven, and it is more than probable that her dream was literally fulfilled, for, as it is related, on Sunday afternoon of the camp meeting she became exceedingly happy, and continued shouting and praising God till she fell dead.

In the spring of '37 we moved into the neighborhood of the school, and occupied a house formerly owned and occupied by Mr. Bell, of revolutionary memory. It is said that Mr. Bell built the church above named, and it generally went by the name of Bell's Meeting-house. It was a log building, not of large dimensions, with a gallery in the end fronting the pulpit, which was generally occupied by the colored people. This was, I think, a free church, for at the time we lived in the neighborhood both the M. E. and the M. P. church had a society in the church with regular preaching, and camp meetings were sometimes held, principally by the M. P. Church. While in this community I lectured frequently on Temperance, at different places.

On the 25th of June, 1837, the Reverend S. Y. McMasters, of the M. P. Church, and myself were solicited to deliver addresses on temperance in the town of New Salem, N. C. We were also requested to write our addresses. We met on 3:00 o'clock, p. m., in the Quaker Church; but brother McMasters did not attend. The meeting was large, and both editors of the Temperance Advocate were present. An extract of the address which I delivered on the occasion was published in the Temperance Advocate and in The Southern Citizen, published in Ashboro by Benjamin Swaim, Esq. Below is the extract verbatim.

* Speech was not enclosed. [Ed.]

In the month of August during this year, I attended a camp-meeting at Salem Church in the northeast portion of Randolph County. Some twelve or thirteen years previous to this time I had attended a camp meeting at this place when a mere youth. The kind treatment with which I was favored by the tent holders made a lasting impression on my mind. These were the Nances, Lewises, Ingrams, Keeams, Woods, and many others. These I remembered with gratitude.

On Saturday in the afternoon when I first stood before the people to preach, I recognized many of these kind friends, though some of their heads had turned gray. This filled me with emotions which almost choked utterance. I read for my text the 16th and 17th verses of the third chapter of Malichi, "Then they that feared the Lord spake often one to another," etc. The excitement was so high that my voice was drown[ed] with the shouting of the people in front and the preachers in the rear. On reaching the preachers tent this unique remark was made by the late Jno. W. Thomas, Esq.,

"Brethren," said he, "I tell you what this afternoon reminded me of. It reminded me of boys hunting rabbits. The dogs had been trailing for a long time, and when they jumped the rabbit, the boys followed and screamed so in every direction that it distracted the dogs and they lost the rabbit." To this one of the preachers replied, "But we did not lose the rabbit, for, though the preacher was disturbed, the object was gained." At this meeting I was strongly solicited by my P. E., the Rev. James Reid, and the preachers generally, to join conference, but could not at that time give a definite answer.

During the autumn of this year, brother Thompson Garrett came all the way from Alamance, then Orange, to request me to attend a camp-meeting of his, to be held almost on the banks of the Haw, at Salem Church. Three different denominations had societies in this church, the M. E. Church, the M. P. Church, and the Presbyterian. To this meeting I consented to go, as it would be almost directly in my way to attend my brother John W.'s wedding, to which I had been invited and consented to go. A young preacher by the name of Jackson who was attending my school at Piney Grove, resolved also to go. I did not reach the camp-ground until Sunday, just as the Presiding Elder was closing the eleven o'clock services. I here formed the acquaintance of the late Hezekiah G. Lee, who was the Presiding Elder, and as we were walking to one of the tents for dinner he remarked to me, "I have a notion of breaking up this camp-meeting tomorrow morning."

"Why," said I.

"Because," said he, "we are doing no good. The Protestant Methodists have just held a camp-meeting here, and never had a single mourner, and we have been here ever since Thursday night and have not had even a grunt. Thompson Garrett," continued he, "is a fool for having appointed a meeting here, for one-half of the people is full of pride, and the other full of prejudice, and the only chance that I can see of doing any good would be to preach to the negroes, and that is not practicable."

I simply replied, "I have come with the intention of remaining till Wednesday morning if the meeting continues, and the result may possibly be better than you expect."

"I would rather see it," said he "than hear tell of it, but I want you to preach for me this afternoon." And here the conversation ended. At the appointed hour I preached, and some five or six penitents presented themselves at the altar. At eleven o'clock on Monday the Presiding Elder preached, nor was it any ordinary effort; it was listened to with profound attention but very little visible effect was produced. At two o'clock, I preached according to appointment, but no extraordinary effect was produced. There were generally at each hour some penitents at the altar but very few converts up to Tuesday. At 11 o'clock Tuesday the Presiding Elder occupied the hour. His sermon was excellent, well planned and well executed, but still there was but very little apparent effect. At 2 o'clock p. m. I preached again, from the 21st verse of 12th chapter of the Gospel by St. John:"Sir, we would see Jesus." The spirit of preaching came upon me and when about two-thirds through the sermon, there was a display of divine power that I have never witnessed before nor since. I felt like my feet would leave the floor of the stand so that I involuntarily grasped the book-board. In looking over the congregation I saw many falling from their seats. Some were shouting aloud, while others were crying as loud for mercy. I called for mourners and it appeared to me as if the whole congregation was trying to get into the altar, and such was their eagerness to get there that they paid but little attention to the manner in which they came, for they fell over the benches or whatever came in their way, and on leaving the stand, the Presiding Elder, who had taken his seat in the altar, said to me, "I have been in the regular work twenty-five years, but have never witnessed such a work nor such a scene." So wonderful was the effect that some of the brethern searched to see how many there were that were not penitents. The result of the investigation was, that only three could be found, and only one of these was in the congregation at the time of preaching. A Mrs. Thompson, who had been seeking religion nineteen years, and was in despair, remained in her tent. The description of another one was an old decrepit lady that remained in some one of the tents. The description of the other, if I heard it, I have forgotten. The work went on, no stopping for supper. The shout of "Glory!" often mingling with cries for mercy. The fame of the meeting spread rapidly among the dense population of the community, and as night drew on the aurora borealis presented the most remarkable phenomenon that had been witnessed for many years. The whole northern hemisphere appeared almost as red as if on fire, and some of the red rays shot up even to the very zenith. This remarkable phenomenon and the extraordinary work which was progressing filled many of the people with wonder and astonishment, and some seemed to think that the day of judgment was at hand.

I never knew a people to manifest such anxiety for preaching. They came to the preachers tent, but in crowds, urging most importunately the Presiding Elder to have preaching, but he told them that was impossible, as no man could preach in such a storm. But this did not satisfy them, for they continued to come, urging their pleas for preaching. A little before midnight, the Presiding Elder asked me if I could preach again, if silence could be procured. I simply replied, "I can try, if you desire it." He then ordered the trumpet to be sounded and proclamation to be made that there would be preaching, if the people could be quiet enough to hear. This was done, and the people became quiet enough to justify the attempt to preach and just at the hour of midnight I commenced preaching, nor do I think I ever witness[ed] such an anxiety to hear. The crowd was immense, there were many more than the seats could contain; though many stood--there were none walking idly about. The effect was overwhelming, and many were the slain of the Lord. Soon after the sermon was over, I was compelled to retire for some rest, but I believe the work went on without intermission during the whole night. Soon the morning dawned--it was Wednesday, and our horses were brought according to order. According to previous arrangement, brother Jackson and I were to meet my brother at twelve o'clock in Hillsboro, which was about seventeen miles distant from the camp-ground. After breakfast, we packed up, bade the preachers farewell, and left the preachers tent, but my horse was missing. I asked some gentlemen standing by if they knew what had become of my horse. One replied, "I do, for I saw a man take him away, and he directed me to tell you that you will not get him today. But give yourself no uneasiness about him, he will be well taken care of and will be here tomorrow morning, shod all round." I then requested brother Jackson to go on and meet my brother and tell him what had occurred and to go with him, and I would next day go a near way and still reach the place in time for the marriage. The work progressed without intermission and many were the converts, but I know not the exact number, but it was suppos[ed] there were more than 200. I gave orders for my horse to be brought next morning by light. I ate breakfast by candle-light, and my horse having been brought according to order, I again bade the preachers farewell, but to my surprise, when I went out to start my horse again was gone and I was informed that I would see him no more that day. Consequently I was compelled to give up going to the wedding, and I continued at the meeting through another day and night. I gave directions to have my horse brought, and not to take him away again, as I had to reach an appointment for preaching, not for a wedding. My horse was brought according to direction and I left the camp-ground on Friday morning, but the meeting still went on. Though I have never heard the exact number of converts, yet the number must have been considerable, and all told I have never witnessed such a work.

As the conference year began to draw to a close, I was frequently solicited, and even importuned, to join the approaching conference. I simply replied to these solicitations that there was one inseparable difficulty in the way--that I had no horse nor had I any money with which to purchase one, nor was I able to procure a suitable outfit. But this difficulty was soon removed, as one brother offered to furnish a horse, and others offered to furnish the money to procure an outfit. Now, as this difficulty was removed, though I did not feel altogether as clear as could be desired, I consented to offer myself to the conference, and as I entertained no doubt of being accepted, I requested my employers to allow me to wind up the school which I was teaching at Piney Grove at the end of nine months, instead of twelve, for which I had consented to teach. This was granted and I held an examination at the close of nine months. Brother Ahi Robins had brought his oldest son, Wm. M. Robins, who had attended. Brother Robins and Lewis Leach, Esq., attended the examination, and as they were highly pleased with the result of the examination, they strongly solicited me to take charge of a school in the vicinity of what is now Trinity College, but to this request I could give no definite answer as I had consented to join Conference the fourth Quarterly meeting, which was to be held at Ebenezer Church, and was now approaching. At this Quarterly Conference I was unanimously recommended as a suitable person to join conference and also for Deacon's orders.

This Annual Conference was held in the town of Greensboro, and was not held till the first day of January, 1838. The reason of this was, the Virginia and North Carolina conference had consented to divide, and form a North Carolina Conference, but this could not be done till after the session of the Virginia Conference, which was held in Petersburg. This was held so late that the first could not be held in '37, but was held early in '38. At the Quarterly conference already referred to brother Jackson was also recommended to the Annual Conference. Brother Jackson and myself reached the conference on Friday evening. Brother Pervis was the preacher in charge and met us kindly, informing me that I had been elected to Deacon's orders, and conducted us to the place assigned for our entertainment. On Sunday I was ordained Deacon by Bishop Morris.

My brother-in-law, John Bond, who was the class leader at Pleasant Garden Church, had become dissatisfied concerning a previous settlement between ourselves. Bond had been notified to attend this conference in order to have the settlement adjusted by a committe of preachers; for he had unadvisedly complained to several preachers that he had reasons to believe that I had wronged him in the settlement. He came to conference on Saturday, but could not be prevailed on to go into the settlement of this difficulty; but promised to return on Monday and attend to it. According to promise he came on Monday, a committee of investigation had been appointed, perhaps, on Saturday, but we could not prevail on him to go into the settlement even on Monday, alleging, perhaps as an excuse, that he was not ready; but as he was starting away on Monday the P. E. met him, and told him if he did not stay and attend to that business that he would have a charge of slander preferred against him. I had given up all hope of getting the matter adjusted and had gone in to hear the missionary address on Monday night, but before the meeting was opened, someone touched [me] and beckon[ed] for me to go to the door. It was Brother Bond who had returned to attend to the settlement. The committee of preachers, which consisted of three, Brother Bond and myself, went into a room in the court house to attend to the settlement, when the previous settlement was laid before the committee, and after a full, somewhat labored and lengthy investigation, the matter was adjusted, and Bond fell several dollars in my debt, instead of I in his. The minutes of the investigation were preserved, and Bond admitted that they were correct, and that the settlement was satisfactory to him.

Early the next morning the P. E. applied to know the result. He was duly informed by the committee and the papers handed to him. He appeared highly pleased and remarked "all is right," or something like it. Soon after the conference had set on Tuesday morning, I was called into the conference room, and requested to make some statements with [respect] to the scientific and literary attainments of brother Jackson, and also in regard to his gifts and graces as a preacher. As soon as I had made these statements, knowing that my recomendation would be presented as soon as Jackson's case was disposed of, the P. E. having presented my recommendations, some preacher inquired whether the difficulty between Bond and me had been settled. To this the P. E. replied, "It has, but I do not positively know." He then asked the conference to indulge him a few minutes till he could see me. He searched but did not find me, returning more confused than ever. Then, on his own responsibility, he withdrew the recommendation. It is proper to remark here that the P. E. had been subject for some time to some occasional obliquities, and during the paroxysms he appeared to have no memory. He told me some two years after that he carried the papers handed him that morning in his hat for twelve months without knowing what they were. As soon as the news of the result reached him, I informed those brethren that were waiting, from the nighborhood of Trinity Collge, that I would teach the school they desired, as I was now satisfied with regard to the call to the work in the conference, and without inquiring of anyone as to the cause of my recommendation being withdrawn, I called for my horse and left, in company with several of the brethren from the neighborhood of Trinity College, who appeared to be highly pleased at the result. This, however, was no doubt caused by their anxiety for the school.

CHAPTER X*

THE ORIGIN OF TRINITY COLLEGE.

* This Chapter was written in 1879 (Editor.)

In the latter part of the year 1837, I was invited by several gentlemen in the neighborhood of Trinity College to teach a school in that community; after some deliberation, I consented.

Early in the spring of 1838, I opened a school in a house known as Brown's Schoolhouse. This house was located about three-quarters of a mile from the place where Trinity College now stands. It was a very inferior building, built of round logs, and covered with common boards. The floor was laid with puncheons and slabs. The chimney was made of wood with a little or no clay in it, tapering up in the form of a partridge trap. The hearth was dirt, and the whole in bad repair; for, when it rained, it was with difficulty that the books and paper could be kept dry. This house was entirely too small to accommodate the students, consequently we were necessitated to erect a bush arbor in front of the south door, and part of the students were under the arbor and part in the house.

As soon as the farmers had laid by their crops, the citizens met in order to select a place to build a better house. A committee was appointed (as well as I recollect) to select a suitable site; and after examining several places, the place where Trinity College now stands was finally chosen as the most convenient situation, and in a few weeks a log building 30 by 20 feet was erected.

Early in the month of August, we moved from Brown's Schoolhouse to the one just completed. We commenced teaching in this new building with sixty-nine students. It was soon ascertained that this building, though much larger and far superior to the one we had just left, was inadequate to accommodate our present number of students.

The first examination held in this new building was in the spring of 1839. Previous to this examination, I had resolved to attempt to establish a permanent institution of learning at this place, based upon an Educational Association, and with a view of reaching the common walks of life with a more thorough education than had been previously afforded them. I consulted one man only, namely, Mr. Jabez Leach with regard to this plan, previous to the examination. During the examination, which lasted two days, I was requested by several citizens to deliver a public lecture; the time fixed upon for it was the second day, immediately after dinner. My theme was, "The importance of establishing a permanent institution of learning of high grade at this place." The lecture having closed, I presented the plan I had previously arranged, which was approved by all. A subscription was then taken up for the purpose of erecting a suitable building, and between three and four hundred dollars were then subscribed. A Committee consisting of three, viz.: General Alexander Gray, J. M. Leach and the writer, was appointed to draft a Constitution and By Laws for the government of the Association. The meeting then adjourned, to meet some ten or twelve days hence, at which time the committee was requested to report.

UNION INSTITUTE EDUCATIONAL SOCIETY.

At the time appointed, the people of the neighborhood met at the place designated in order to organize an Educational Society, and to do such other things as might be deemed important in advancing the interest of the Institution. Up to this, the Institution had been a "local habitation," but no name. The Principal of the School was requested to give it a name. The name which he gave it was Union Institute, which name it held till it became Normal College. The Institution was located between two populous neighborhoods, the one on the south called Hopewell, the inhabitation of which were generally Methodists; the other on the north, Springfield, whose inhabitants were principally Quakers. The object in naming it Union Institute was to unite these two neighborhoods in the interest of the school. This was happily effected.

The committee appointed to draft a Constitution reported; each member had drawn a draft separately, and from these several drafts a Constitution had been formed and was now adopted. The Association thus formed, was denominated Union Institute Educational Society. General Alexander Gray was chosen President; J. M. Leach, Esq., Secreetary. The names of the other officers [are] not recollected. The Principal of the school (B. York) was requested to act as Agent for the Society.

The Society resolved to erect a frame building fifty feet by twenty-five, one-story, with an eight feet passage through the center, dividing the building into two rooms of equal size, each room to have two fire-places. The rooms were entered from doors opening from the passage. A building committee was now chosen to carry into effect the resolution of the Society.

The Constitution provided that the Principal and all the officers of the Society should be elected annually by ballot.

This organization was the beginning or origin of what is now Trinity College.

The fourth of July, 1839, was set apart by the Educational Society for laying the corner-stone of the proposed building. On that occasion a large concourse of people assembled and were addressed by Julian E. Leach, Esq., J. M. Leach, Esq., and the principal of the institution.

This was a day of feasting and gladness, full of hope and prospect.

The work was soon commenced and before cold weather the building was completed, and the school removed into it, and the former building was occupied by the Principal and his family. The Institution was now in a flourishing condition, and in the new building the students found ample room and excellent accommodation. Sometime in the spring of 1840, date not recollected, the Union Institute Educational Society held its annual meeting. At this meeting two candidates, the present Principal and Rev. Franklin Harris, offered their services as principal. The election resulted in the re-election of the former by an almost unanimous vote, only one against.

In the spring of 1841, the Educational Society held its third annual meeting. Two candidates again offered their services, namely, the former principal and Mr. John D. Clancy. The former Principal was re-elected by a very large majority (only two vote for Clancy).

During this year the Rev. Braxton Craven, a young man of some nineteen or twenty, entered the school, and soon after was employed as an assistant teacher, and continued to officiate in that capacity till the resignation of the Principal. The school continued to flourish; the number of students never falling under fifty, but it generally far exceeded that number.

Early in the year 1842, I (the principal) was elected the Principal of Clemonsville High School, male and female; and, for reasons which will be given hereafter, accepted the position. In due time notice was given to the Educational Society that I would not be a candidate at their next annual meeting.

According to the arrangement made between Mr. Craven and myself, he was to go with me to Clemonsville and still officiate as assistant teacher, but as the time drew near for the election of another Principal, and no candidate offered his services, some of the leading members of the Society inquired of me as to the fitness of Mr. Craven for the principalship. Though I was anxious for him to go with me, yet such were his studious habits and his ability to learn, that I willingly recommended him as a suitable person for that position; consequently he was chosen principal at the ensuing election and has continued there from that time till the present (June 20, 1876), except two years during the war, during which time he was stationed in Raleigh, Edenton Street Church.

So faithfully and ably has Mr. Craven discharged the duties thus devolved upon him that the most sanguine expectations concerning him have been more than realized, and Trinity College today ranks among the best literary institutions of the country.

THE ASPIRANT TEACHERS.

Mr. Isaiah Ingold was my first assistant teacher. He ofciated in this capacity for the greater part of 1838. Miss Irena Leach, now Mrs. Braxton Craven, succeeded him, and continued to render such aid as was needed, till Mr. Craven was employed in that capacity, as has already been noticed. The school during its academical career was both male and female.

WHY I LEFT UNION.

There were reasons sufficiently strong for my resignation to satisfy my own mind that the course pursued was proper, though I do not know that it would be of any practical utility to the public for these reasons to be disclosed. But because I could not hold my position any longer was not, as some have intimated, any part of the reason why I left; for I was repeatedly and strongly urged to continue; nor was it a decline of patronage, for this was not the case. The work of the four years spent at Union Institute was truly onerous, my faculties, both mental and physical having been taxed to their utmost capacity. I not only had a large school to superintend, but, also as agent, had the funds to collect for carrying on the work, and, then, I was hearing recitations on four subjects which I had not studied, consequently I was necessitated to prepare at night for the recitations of the next day. It was there and then that my vision began to fail, and from that time till now I have had to contend with defective vision or total blindness.

I have written this hasty sketch entirely from memory, having no statistics at hand; consequently there may be some slight errors as to terms and dates, but I believe the general statements are substantilly true. There may be found, I suppose, in the archives of Trinity College, the Secretary's book, which contains the proceedings of Union Institute Society from its first organization in 1839 till my resignation.

CHAPTER XI.

CLEMONSVILLE--ITINERANT TEACHING--OLIN HIGH SCHOOL--
BLINDNESS--CAREER AS AUTHOR--YORK COLLEGIATE INSTITUTE.

Early in the year '42 I was elected principal of Clemonsville High School, male and female, and after some deliberation accepted; consequently I wound up my business at Union Institute at the close of the spring session, resigning my position in the school as principal, refusing a re-election, though earnestly solicited and recommended Dr. Craven, then a young man about twenty years of age as a suitable person to take my place which I had resigned. Early in the month of April, I opened my first session at Clemonsville; the session was prosperous, opening with about forty students. Near the close of this session the Asthma, with which I had been afflicted for several years, seemed to reach its climax, insomuch that my life was despaired of by my family physicians, their remedies all having failed. They had used the most active emetics known to the medical science, but without effect. But a simple remedy succeeded, and appeared to save my life. Mrs. York, learning my danger, drew hot embers from the fireplace, and sprinkling water on them and wrapping them up in a cloth, applied it to my breast and stomach. This seemed to impart sufficient vitality to enable the emetics to operate, giving me a speedy relief.

During the session I generally preached twice on every Sabbath, and not infrequently I was called out of town to preach funeral sermons on other days. I generally preached in the country in the day, and in town at night. At the close of the first session my health was such it was thought best for me to take some recreation in traveling, during which time I attended a camp meeting in Rowan County at a place called South River Campground. From Mocksville we were accompanied by the Rev. Baxter Clegg, the principal of Mocksville Academy. He was very kind to us and offered much assistance, as our horse was baulky and often refused to pull. We reached the campground about twelve o'clock Saturday and weak and fatigued as I was, I was appointed to preach on Saturday evening; but should doubtless have failed had I not been relieved by a heavy shower of rain. But I rested better than usual on the following night, and was so refreshed that I preached at eleven o'clock on Sunday to a very large audience. The attention of the audience was unusually good, and the effect was so powerful, that it is said by a close observer that there was not a dry eye in the congregation. As I came out of the stand, I was met by a well-dressed gentleman, who introduced himself to me as the High Sheriff of the county. He remarked to me, "I have been a very wicked man, but your sermon has enabled me to resolve to be a better man. I want you to pray for me." On the next day when I preached he presented himself at the altar as a penitent, and on the following day professed conversion. He urged me importunately to go to Salisbury and preach. I consented, though my health was not good. I went and continued to preach for ten days--not without effect, for the Lord was certainly with us to bless the word. Salisbury at this time was only an appointment on a circuit, with but a small membership. Soon after, it became a station, and has so continued ever since. The time was now drawing near when the next session must open. We returned to Clemonsville with my health somewhat improved. The second session opened well. There were several boarders from Salisbury, Germanton and many other places. Miss Angelina Clemons was my assistant during this session. During the session a very interesting debating club was organized, composed of citizens and students; not only citizens of the town but also of the sur rounding country. We also organizeed a temperance society which prospered during my stay in Clemonsville. Regular meetings were held and addresses were frequently delivered, and much good no doubt was the result. My plan of preaching was about as during the former session. The session closed a little before Christmas. The classes were examined before the trustees. We also had some declamations and dialogues with which the trustees and all others as far as I know were well plased. After a vacation of some two weeks, early in January, we opened the spring session. The session opened prosperously. During this session the Rev. Henry Speck, P. C., of the Davidson circuit, bought a lot in Clemonsville, and moved his family, for educational purposes; also the Rev. Jno. W. Lewis, (who) was the P. C. of the Stokes Circuit, to which Clemonsville belonged. This session closed early in June. We had a two days' examination for the various classes in the school. We also had an exhibition of no little interest at night. Complimentary remarks were made by several gentlemen at the close; but no regular address or sermon. This was seldom done in those days, if ever. During the vacation I visited various places, and attended some two or three camp meetings.

We had generally much preaching in the chapel by brother Lewis, the P. C., by brother Speck occasionally, by brother Joshua Bethel, a superannuated preacher, who lived in the place. I generally preached every Sunday night and we frequently has sermons from preachers who were transient visitors;

but notwithstanding all this preaching the people appeared to be unusually hard, though they were a churchgoing people; hence the preachers came to the conclusion that they were gospel hardened, and that preaching would only aggravate their condemnation. Hence, in council they resolved to stop preaching, except the P. C. must necessarily preach at his regular appointment. I however was not in the council and was ignorant of the result of their deliberations, being out of town at the time. It was agreed that Brother Bethel should preach on Sunday following at eleven o'clock, and inform the people of their resolution to cease preaching to them, believing it would prove a curse instead of a blessing. On the same sunday I preached to a congregation in the country. As I rode into town that evening, I was hailed by Brother Bethel, who informed me of the resolution which the preachers had gone into, and advised me also to cease preaching to them, and not to have the bell rung that evening, as he had told the people there would be no more preaching, only by the P. C. In reply I said, "brother Bethel, I cannot go into that arrangement, as I have learned my lesson differently. I understand from the bible that we as watchmen are to cry aloud and spare not--to preach to the people whether they hear or forbear, and to be instant in season and out of season." Brother Bethel replied "Then you will preach to no purpose, and your work will be in vain."

The bell was rung at the proper time, and an unusual congregation assembled. The chapel was almost literally packed. I took for my text, "Owe no man anything but to love one another." The audience listened with unusual interest. Towards the close of my sermon I remarked, "I understand that the other preachers have given you up, believing that preaching would be a curse instead of a blessing and I suppose they were sincere and honest; but this I cannot do, I will not do. I will not cease preaching and praying for you till I know that the door of mercy is closed against you." This moved the whole audience, and a powerful revival broke out, which resulted in perhaps one hundred converts. The preachers, though a little slow, gradually entered into the work and all went on harmoniously.

The fall session of '43 opened early in August. At the opening of this session, Mr. Erasmus Burkit entered school and became my assistant teacher for some three sessions. The school still flourished, and was perhaps fuller this session than it had been at any previous one. The girls and boys recited in separate rooms--the girls reciting to me and most of the boys to Mr. Burkit. Some of the trustees according to an arrangement made by themselves, visited the school every Friday afternoon when the students were briefly examined on their week's work. This had a happy effect, as it excited the students to greater diligence and to make greater efforts. I preached as I had formerly done, and delivered some temperance addresses or lectures. The fall session closed as usual a little before Christmas. On the 1st of January, '44, the spring session opened and the school was still in a flourishing condition. During this session I formed a grammar class at Midway, which I met every other Saturday. I also formed another at Farmington Davie County so that my time was fully occupied teaching every day in the week, except Sunday, and on that day I generally preached twice. This session closed on the first of June, and the examinations were very interesting and highly approved. During the greater portion of this year the Methodist church was much excited. The General Conference which met in New York sometime in May, after a spirited debate on the question of slavery made arrangements for separation into two General Conferences, and as the terms of this separation had to be laid by the P. E. before a Quarterly Conference of each circuit and station much debate and excitement prevailed; but the division was effected. After a vacation of some two months, the fall session of '44 opened; the school was still in a flourishing condition; no radical change was made in the regulation of my preaching during the session; but my health was bad, and sometimes my whole family was down with the chills and fever at the same time. Chills and fever, and bilious fever were very common both in the village and the surrounding country. My vision was also rapidly failing. A little before Christmas the session closed as usual.

Sometime in the autumn of this year ('44) Rev. Henry Speck P. C. of the Davidson circuit appointed a camp-meeting to be held at Midway church one of the appointments on his circuit. He said to me, "brother York you must without fail help me at this camp meeting, you and I will be the P. E. Be certain to be there on Friday evening, and make your arrangements so that you can remain during the meeting." I was there on Friday evening; Brother Speck was not. He was at Lexington very sick, and on Saturday evening we received the sad intelligence that he was dead. This news caused much sorrow in the camp. The management of the meeting consequently fell on me; the meeting was a success. So great was the revival that the meeting was protracted till Thursday morning, and, as I now recollect, there were some fifty or more converts, and quite a number joined the church. The circuit remained unoccupied during the balance of the year.

Early in January ('45) the seventh session was opened as prosperously as ever, and closed early in June. With a single exception we had the severest drought that I ever knew. The corn crop on upland was almost an entire failure. The fall session opened early in August as usual. My grammar class still continued at Midway with increasing numbers. My health had become so bad and my vision [was] failing so fast that I was advised to give up the schoolroom and reading as much as possible. I had almost reached the conclusion to give up teaching; but I knew not what to follow as a livelihood. The present session having closed, I consented to continue one more session. The ninth session, ('46) opened early in January, with but little increase or diminution of students. After much deliberation and consultation I resolved to resign at the end of the session, and there seemed to be but one path open for me, and that was to adopt an itinerant system of teaching. I consulted with many of my friends with regard to the probability of success in my new plan of teaching, and the general expression was "It looks like it might succeed; but it is an un-trodden track--an untried system; hence it would be safer and more likely to succeed to continue in the ordinary system of teaching." But this appeared to me to be the next door to the impossible; for my health was so feeble and my vision so bad that let the consequences be what they might, I must leave the schoolroom. The trustees were very unwilling to give me up, and at the close of the session, they offered to double my wages if I would continue; but this appeared to me impracticable; hence, I resigned my position as principal of the school, with no expectation of ever engaging in a regular school again.

Soon after we went to Clemonsville, I observed that the religious instruction of the slave population was wholly neglected. There were no seats prepared for them in the chapel; consequently I never saw a negro there except nurses, and they were always outdoors with the children, of whom they had charge. With this arrangement I was much dissatisfied consequently I visited every slave holder in the village and reasoned with each one separately. I endeavored to convince them that they were responsible for the religious instruction of their own slaves, and that while we were paying money to preach to the negroes in Africa we were utterly neglecting those over whom we had immediate control. They appeared to feel the force of the argument, but did not know how to remedy the evil. I told them that though my work was laborious I would preach to the negroes every other Sunday at three o'clock P. M. To this their owners readily consented. As soon as this arrangement was known, they came from all the surrounding country even to the distance of eight or ten miles. The chapel was literally packed to its utmost capacity. Soon a gracious revival broke out, and of the fruits of this revival a class was formed of some thirty-five or forty members, and I was appointed their leader, and I officiated in this capacity as long as I remained with them, and I never knew a more appreciative people. They seemed to take pleasure in doing anything they could for me.

After a week or two's rest, I set out with a view to put into operation the plan previously formed. From the proficiency made by the classes of Midway and Farmington, with which I spent only one day in two weeks, I was fully convinced of the practicability and utility of this method of imparting instruction, and the only difficulty now that remained in my mind was whether I could convince the people of what I so firmly believed. In order to get before the people I sent out appointments in various places, villages, towns and the country, that at a specified time I would deliver a lecture on education. The people generally turned out well and I very seldom failed to form a class wherever I lectured. In this way, I formed a circuit of classes or grammar schools which required two weeks to visit each class once a day, though sometimes where the classes were large I spent two days. In most places where I had classes in the day I lectured on Elocution at night, and generally preached several times on each round. The people generally were highly pleased with the plan and very readily supported the schools, though some few opposed. The lecturing on Elocution and Grammar and the preaching produced no little excitement in the communities, so much so that one very intelligent lady sought an introduction to me where I was attending a camp-meeting and said as she approached the door of the tent in which I was sitting, "I have come to see the man who has turned the world upside down." I followed this plan exclusively for about five years, and I am fully impressed with the belief that under Providence I accomplished more for education and religion than in any other period of my life of the same length; for hundreds were brought into contact with education, and acquired a thirst for it, and acquired the habit of studying at home, who could not obtain an education in the ordinary way, and also many were influenced to go to the regular schools of the country, and even to college; for as this gave them a taste for study and a love of learning, they were not satisfied with smaller attainments. I also preached more frequently than I could have done in any regular station or school. In the year '48 I preached 178 sermons, and if I preached as many each year as I did this year, I preached 890 sermons in the five years.

In traveling round the circuit of schools in two weeks, I generally had to travel about two hundred miles, and generally every day was occupied in teaching the classes. The

time occupied in teaching was from nine o'clock in the morning to three and a half or four in the evening and two thirds of the night at least were occupied either in teaching Elocution, Grammar or preaching. I generally preached twice on Sunday, and sometimes three times; but notwithstanding the immense labor which I had to perform, my general health rapidly improved. My pecuniary income was greater than it ever had been before. During the winter of '46 and '47 we left Clemonsville, and moved to Jonesville, Jonesville being nearer the center of my work, a much more healthy location, and also there was a good academical school permanently located at this place. During the year '47, I attended several camp-meetings, most of which lay within the boundary of my work. At some of these meetings there was an unusual work. At Snow Creek in Iredell County, the P. C. Brother John Tillet said there were something over three hundred converts, and not a few of them prominent citizens. At this meeting, I preached four times: at Harmony Hill, a union camp-meeting, about one hundred and fifty professed faith in Christ. At this camp-meeting I preached five times. In the latter part of the year '48 we left Jonesville, and moved to Iredell County and lived at a place then called James Crossroads, now Keatons. In the latter part of this year I attended a session of the N. C. Conference, held at Danville, Va., and was there ordained Elder by Bishop Capers.

Early in the spring of '49 I visited for the first time Lenoir, the county seat of Caldwell County, and formed a large class both in grammar and Elocution, and subsequently formed classes in various portions of this county, also in Alexander and Burke.

At the close of the first twenty days' session we commenced a protracted meeting. We had Rev. R. L. Abernethy and two Local Preachers living in the town, namely, Brothers Pevet and Hevlen, [but] the preacher in charge Rev. Paul Kistler, was absent. We commenced preaching on Saturday night and at eleven o'clock service on Sunday, a very gracious revival broke out--not less than twenty-five or thirty penitents were at the altar. The meeting continued through the balance of the week; there were many converts but the precise number not recollected--in truth, the town was almost revolutionized. At the opening of the next session there were sixty-two students--more than I could well manage.

In passing from Snow Creek to Moriah Church, a night class was formed at Nesbit's and Turner's tanyard. This night class was the opening wedge to the establishment of the school called New Institute; several years later the name was changed to Olin High School. At the close of this night school a day class was formed in the district school house, in the immediate neighborhood. During this school I was frequently and strongly solicited by the citizens of the neighborhood generally to aid them in establishing a permanent institution of high grade in that vicinity; but I did not feel willing to abandon my itinerating system; but importunity finally led me to consent to devote a part of my time to the building of the institution desired, and in the latter part of the year '50, the neighborhood held a meeting at the district schoolhouse with a view to effect a permanent organization upon which the institution was to be based. An educational association was organized and regularly officered. I was elected agent, and for acting in that capacity I was to receive 25 per cent of the money raised. The payment of five dollars constituted a membership for life. The site finally selected for the location of the institution is the site now occupied by Olin High School. I had some seven or eight classes still on hand, but immediately commenced operations as agent, devoting all the time I could to it, and was very successful, for the people generally approved of the plan, and readily subscribed.

In the latter part of the year '50 we left the Crossroads and occupied a house in the vicinity of New Institute. By order of the educational association, three houses were to be erected as early as possible, one for a school-room, and two for Professors; but at this time no house was completed, nor were they even commenced. But early in the year '51, building was commenced, and rapidly prosecuted. Two gentlemen, Messrs. Lassen Nesbit and Chapman Turner, donated 11 acres of land to the institution, which was laid off into half acre lots, except the lots for the institution and professors, which were sold at public auction and the proceeds appropriated to the institution. The fourth of July, '51, was a high day for New Institute. A public dinner was given to all present. In the forenoon the Declaration of Independence was read by Col. Jones of Williamsburg, and an address on the fourth of July, by Quincey Sharpe, Esq., of Statesville, and in the afternoon the people were addressed by Rev. B. York, on the subject of education, and a liberal subscription was lifted.

On the 7th of June, '51, I was elected Principal of the school. The work had now so far advanced that it was believed the school could be opened in September, and on 2nd August of the same year the Rev. Baxter Clegg was elected Professor of Latin and Greek. The first session opened in September or October, with about forty students. There were sub-agents in different portions of the State. Rev. Minton Connelly was elected agent and collector; but it was soon found to be absolutely necessary for me to continue in the agency, as money came in too slowly for successfully carrying on the work; hence while I still held my position as principal of the school, I was urged to travel as agent, while Rev. B. Clegg acted as Principal of the school. The number of students continued to increase, and building went on rapidly. It was soon found that it was necessary for Professor Clegg to have an assistant. Mr. John Kinion was elected Professor of Modern Languages and Mathematics. The spring session of '52 opened with about 100 students, and the numbers continued to increase till they reached the number of 146. After I had wound up my circuit schools, no more were formed in that way, though I continued teaching classes both in this State and South Carolina in connection with my work as agent. In the summer of '52, Rev. James Pastell came from South Carolina with the express purpose of getting me to go to that state to teach grammar classes. I went with him and a large one was formed at Armenia Church, Chester County. This was the first class taught in this state. The result of the teaching made a strong impression, and I was solicited to return by several gentlemen in Yorkville, and in the autumn of the same year I visited Yorkville, and formed classes both for the day and night, and continued a large portion of the winter of '52 and '53 in the same place. I did my teaching without a book, using the blackboard and slates, for I could find no book that would suit my method of teaching, and while in Yorkville I commenced writing, with a view to publishing a book on English Grammar, and wrote about fifty pages of foolscap, which was all I ever wrote with my own hand. In every place where I taught scholars went to New Institute, and there were some thirty boarders from South Carolina in the spring session of '53.

While I was in South Carolina teaching classes, I preached frequently; for I attended two camp-meetings, and I also lectured in several places in favor of the institution of learning which I was representing. Nor did I lecture in vain; for the people generally gave liberally, though the itinerant preachers, or at least some of them, did not favor the enterprise, because the institution was located in North Carolina, and too many of them were prejudiced against the North Carolina Conference; because a large portion of the territory in North Carolina occupied by the South Carolina Conference had been recently by the act of the General Conference transferred to the North Carolina Conference. One of the principal pleas which I offered as a reason why they should support this institution was that young men in indigent circumstances preparing for the ministry, irrespective of the church relations, would receive their education free of tuition. While I was lecturing and teaching in Yorkville, I attended a session of the South Carolina Conference held in Sumpterville. While there I had abundant evidence of the prejudices entertained against the North Carolina Conference, for, though I asked for but one-half hour to address the conference on the subject of my agency, it was promptly refused, and though the committee on Divine service was frequently and strongly solicited to appoint me [to] preach at some hour during the conference, they peremptorily refused, saying, "We have preachers enough of our own to fill the hours without calling on a North Carolinian." Yet there were several honorable exceptions to this treatment; for there were some twelve or fifteen who subscribed liberally to the institution.

I returned from South Carolina early in the spring of '53, and, having been solicited by a gentleman whom I met on the cars, to visit Rutherford County and lecture and form classes, in a few days after reaching home I set out for that county. I lectured in Rutherfordton, the county seat, and formed a night class of some twenty students. I also visited Gray's Chapel some seven or eight miles from town. I also formed a class there of some twenty or more students--the two classes paid something over $10.00 per day. After the close of these classes, I returned home; but my vision had so failed that it was with much difficulty that I could travel even on horseback, and when I forded the Catawba river, I could not tell in what direction the horse was going. The number of students had so increased that the association was compelled to erect another house for instruction as large as the first building. Now there was sufficient room to accommodate 150 or 200 students. In a few days after my return from Rutherford the commencement of the school came off. The attendance was large and much interest was manifested in the school. Before I left Rutherford, I promisd to return and teach a class at Thoms Schoolhouse, and as my vision was now too defective to travel alone, my son Watson went with me, and continued till the session closed. He then returned home taking the buggy and horse with him. Another class was formed at Baptist church, but a large number of the class at the schoolhouse joined at the church.

Brother Gartrell, a local preacher from the State of Georgia, who had attended the class at the schoolhouse joined at the church, also his wife. We boarded together some four miles from the church, and as he had a horse and carriage, he conveyed me to the school and back. I had written before the school closed for Mrs. York to meet me at Rock Spring in Lincoln County. The class closed on Thursday and the meeting commenced on the Friday night following. Soon after reaching there Mrs. York arrived. After the camp-meeting had closed we set out for Gray's Chapel where I had engaged to teach another class. But on the way we stopped at another camp-meeting at Center Camp-ground. We found Brother Gray and his family, with whom I had boarded, encamped on the ground. As soon as the meeting had closed we proceeded to the chapel, where a very large class of nearly forty students was formed. The class was so large that I found it necessary to employ an assistant teacher. Sixteen students boarded in the same house with us. I continued at Gray's Chapel forty days. The class was large and very interesting,--several teachers were in the class. Miss Matilda Smith, daughter of the late Campbell Smith, of Rutherford, was my assistant teacher. She was about sixteen years old, but had attended two grammar classes previously. She was unusually talented and amiable as she was talented; she subsequently was generally engaged in teaching; but died before she was thirty; "death loves a shining mark."

While I was teaching this class at the Chapel, I was requested by certain gentlemen to visit Spartanburg, South Carolina, as they would insure me a good class. At the close of the class, I went, and some five or six students went with me. This was in the latter part of October, '53. A class was immediately formed, and I continued there forty days, and while here I became totally blind. Though my vision had been long declining, yet the close was sudden and unexpected; for, on Saturday night, as I was preparing to preach on the following day, I was reading and writing till eleven o'clock and when I awoke next morning, I was blind. This was one of the darkest days of my life, and, for the first time in my life I preached without seeing the congregation. I knew not what to do nor what I could do; but the thing which troubled me most was the thought that my literary career was ended, and the grammar which I was preparing for publication would never see the light.

During the time that my vision was declining, I passed through many remarkable optical illusions. At first an object appeared double, and I was constantly deceived with regard to the distance of objects. Next, the objects appeared triple, and then quadruple, then passing over the numbers 5, 6 and 7, one object appeared as 8. The moon looked like eight distinct moons; four were entirely distinct and separate, the others were touching at certain points and forming certain angles. At one time a candle or lamp, seen at the distance of the diameter of a common sitting room, formed a circular flame nearly as large as the circumference of a small spinning wheel--the circular flame was perfect except one small arc was dark at the lower edge of the circumference, and in the area of the circle, there appeared to be scattered through its surface flames of the candle, forming every kind of angle, and the circumference of the circle increased as the distance increased. During this illusion I preached at several camp-meetings. At night the scene was magnificent, and beggars description. Perhaps a hundred circles of fire of different diameters appeared at the same time, and each fire-stand on the outside made a large brilliant circle, enveloping the whole congregation in an apparent flame of fire, and the people appeared to be sitting, and walking and standing enveloped in circles of fire. The last illusion was the most distressing of all for every object which I saw appeared to touch my face, and the ground on which I walked appeared to be standing perpendicularly immediately before my face. This was worse than total blindness but was of short duration.

A few days before Christmas, the last session of the class closed, and we set out for home from which I had been absent for more than six months. On arriving at home I found every person excited with a grand enterprise in which the association had engaged. A three-story brick building, 100 by 80 feet was to be erected, and indeed had already been let out. Mr. Azer Shell, of Lenoir, had bidden it off at $9,999.00. To meet these expenditures they had negotiated a loan of $10,000.00, but even this failed to cover the expenses. A gentleman from Stanley County, who had come there some ten months previous, with a capital of some $3,000.00, had purchased a lot and small house, and had made additions to it sufficient to accommodate some eight or ten boarders, and agreed to erect a house to board girls at a cost of some $1,500. In short all appeared to be looking through glasses of great magnifying powers. As soon as a meeting of the Association could be called, I gave them my opinion with regard to that entire enterprise--that though I was not a prophet nor the son of a prophet, it would seriously damage the school if it did not ruin it. "Oh, no! this is looking at the dark side of the picture." Professor Clegg had told them that instead of getting one dollar, they would get ten, and instead of ten, a hundred, and instead of a hundred, a thousand.

As I was now blind and knew not what course to pursue, I resigned my connection with the institution, both as agent and Principal, and gave up my book. A committee was appointed to investigate the book of subscriptions and report. They reported $8,000.00 subscription, and thought that $7,000 were perfectly good. This report appeared to encourage the Association very much. Twenty-five per cent of this belonged to me as agent. They appointed a collector with instructions to collect as fast as the nature of the case would admit. In a short time, they called another meeting in my absence, with barely a quorum, and, with one fell stroke, struck down the constitution, and established the school on the old trustee system. According to the former constitution everyone who paid his dollar was constituted a member of the Association, and in virtue of the membership had a right to a vote in all the business transactions relating to the school. This last act, changing the constitution, gave almost universal dissatisfaction nor would scarcely a member pay his subscription. In this way they not only lost some five or six thousand dollars, but caused me to lose some $1,700.00. Nor was this all, for they lost a very large fraction of their patronage, for, after the building had been completed, and the school moved into it they had only forty students, having lost more than 100 students. Affairs now appeared gloomy. Professor Lander was employed as principal and Professor Clegg as agent; and for his services they agreed to pay his expenses and $1,200 per year. He signally failed as an agent, nor did he collect one-third enough to pay himself, nor did the institution ever regain its former prosperity, and in a short time a mortgage was given on all the school property for the debt which they had contracted, and it finally fell into the hands of the man who had loaned the money, nor did he ever get the money he had loaned. Not only did the institution fail, but nearly all who were actively engaged in the enterprise.

CAREER AS AN AUTHOR.

In the year '52, by order of the educational association, I published a book in pamphlet form containing the constitution and by-laws of the association, the improved system of teaching, etc. In the year '56, by request of the York Col. Association, I published another book in pamphlet form similar to the one previously published, only more voluminous. In the year '54 I published the first edition of York's English Grammar, consisting of

2,500 copies. It was published in Salisbury, and printed by J. J. Brunner, editor of the Salisbury Watchman. In '59 an enlarged, stereotyped edition, consisting of 1,000 copies, was published in New York, but by neglect of Mr. Pomeroy my publisher the plates were lost, which cost me several hundred dollars, as the War came on, and all communication with the North was cut off. In the year '60 the first edition of the Common School Grammar, consisting of 5,000 copies, was published in the city of Raleigh, printed by Mr. Gorman, Editor of the Spirit of the Age. In the year '62 the third edition of the High School Grammar, consisting of 2,500 [copies] was published in the city of Raleigh, printed by Mr. Gorman. Sometime during the War a second edition of the Common School Grammar was published in the city of Raleigh, by Dr. Branson, my publisher--number of copies not recollected. In the year '79, the fourth edition of the High School Grammar, revised and enlarged, was published in the city of Raleigh, printed by Mr. John Nichols, 1,000 copies. In the year '80 the third edition revised and enlarged, [of the Common School Grammar] was published by Edwards, Broughton & Co. In the year '84 the fourth edition of the Common School Grammar, consisting of 2,000 copies, was published in Raleigh by Edwards, Broughton & Co. In the year '73, the Man of Business and Railroad Calculator, a book containing applied Arithmetic and Legal Forms, was published in the city of Raleigh. An unpublished manuscript, consisting of Dialogues, Colloquies and short speeches, adapted to schools and colleges is in the possession of my son, Rev. B. A. York.

    While I was preparing the English Grammar for publication a number of young men and some young ladies in the school urged me to give them lessons in English grammar, stating that they could not learn the grammar as it was taught in the regular school. I consented to give them two lessons in the day; one in the forenoon and one in the afternoon, one hour long; and some studying Latin, with a view to studying the law, applied for the same privilege, which was granted. Hence three hours in the day were occupied in teaching; the balance of the time was devoted to writing. To this teaching, Professor Clegg objected, and tried to prevent it, but could not. He said nothing to me about it, but threatened expulsion to the students if they persisted, but this also was unavailing, for the students continued firm in their purpose, and at the close of the session of the regular school, some twenty students remained in order to go through a thorough course in English Grammar, and a class of thirty was formed for a term of thirty days. Notwithstanding this teaching hindered me in the prosecution of my work, yet it was a great pecuniary relief. During the early part of my blindness, the people sincerely sympathized with my condition, and almost every place I preached or lectured, more or less donations were made, and the session of the North Carolina Conference held at Pittsboro, in the winter of '53 and '54, sent me a donation of $104.00 to aid in purchasing me a home. But the more and longer the people became acquainted with my condition, the less they were inclined to give. Hence I was soon thrown upon my own resources, and even now (1886) I succeed better in traveling among strangers than among familiar friends; for, "a prophet is not without honor save in his own country and among his own kin." But under a kind Providence and in a great measure by dint of my own efforts, I have succeeded in raising and educating a large family, and though almost the whole of my public life I have been seriously afflicted, and have suffered much from Asthma, and have occasionally suffered much from other diseases, my health is better now at the age of 82 than in the days of many years long gone by.

After I had become blind, and had resigned my connection with the Olin High School, as it was afterwards called, and the people expected no further advantages from me, they seemed to forget their former promises; for they promised me and Mrs. York, that, if I would go in with them and build up this school I would never lack a home, nor would my favors ever be forgotten. I was necessarily compelled to travel, and it was necessary the most of the time for Mrs. York to be with me, and for several months we had all left home, and while we were all away we hired a gentleman with a small family to take care of our property. Strange as it may seem, those who had been most urgent on me to abandon my regular business, and aid in building up the school, endeavored to get this man to give up the house, and threatened him with the law if he did not. He wrote me with regard to what was going on. On receiving the news, Mrs. York left and went home--had she not done this the probability it that they would have got possession of the house. It has long been said that republics are ungrateful. The same may be predicated of schools.

The first edition of the Grammar having been published, which had exhausted all the money I had on hand, leaving me some hundred dollars in debt, it became necessary for me to leave home, and try what I could do in the way of teaching, lecturing and preaching. As it appeared necessary for Mrs. York to go with me, it was thought advisable to break up housekeeping for a while. All the children except the youngest, that was an infant, were placed in the care of my daughter, Mrs. Elliott. We left home in the latter part of the year '54, and went to Union Factory, now Randleman, where I preached several times and lectured and formed a class both for day and night. The night class was especially large; consequently I needed help, and immediately sent for Watson, my oldest son. We continued teaching in Union nearly all the winter of '54 and '55. Winding up here, I went to Franklinsville, and formed classes for both day and night, and we continued teaching some 50 days, at the close of which it became necessary for Mrs. York to return home, and I set out in company with my son Watson, preaching and lecturing in various places. Among other places we visited South Lowell Academy. There the Principal, Rev. Mr. Bagley, and others urged me to return and deliver the annual address at the approaching commencement. To this I consented, and returned home. During my stay at home I was solicited by several gentlement from Rocky Spring neighborhood to assist them in building up an institution of learning. After much consultation I gave my consent which, as the sequel will show, resulted in a considerable disadvantage in a pecuniary point of view. At the appointed time I returned to South Lowell to deliver the annual address. While at the commencement I was invited by the Principal and others to return at the opening of the next session and give a full course of instruction on English Grammar and Elocution. I was also invited by Professor Baily, Principal of Red Mountain Seminary, to give the young ladies of the Seminary a full course of instruction in English Grammar. I consented to return and give the desired instruction in both seminaries, which were only about four miles distant from each other. Again I returned home, and during the interim I lectured at Rocky Spring Church and formed an educational Association, and took up a subscription of something over $500.00. The Association agreed, if I would take charge of the school, that they would build a good house, and give it to me as a donation. At the time appointed for the opening of the sessions of these schools, I, in company with my son, returned and fell in with the Quarterly meeting at South Lowell, and preached on Saturday night of the meeting, when a revival of no ordinary extent broke out, and I continued preaching through the whole of the next week, with several other preachers. Robert O. Burton was the P. E., and brother Avent, P. C. During this meeting I heard Dr. Mangum preach his first sermon, from "This their way is their folly."

As notice had been given of the lectures that were to be given, several teachers came in--one or two from Fayetteville, and one from Randolph. I continued here teaching, giving the lessons the same day at both places, and both day and night for some six weeks, and was abundantly successful. Besides the pay for the teaching, the young men of South Lowell made a donation of some forty or forty-five dollars, and the young ladies at Red Mountain between twenty and thirty dollars; besides I received donations from various others, and during the time I preached at various places, and at one place where I preached on Saturday and Sunday at a protracted meeting, on Sunday a collection was taken up in my favor, amounting to about $34.00.

While lecturing at these schools, I was strongly urged by the gentlemen of the neighborhood to remain with them. They offered to furnish me with a house and lot, and support my family entirely for no other remuneration than my preaching. To this liberal offer I could not consent; because my hands were fettered--I had previously promised the people at Rocky Spring to go there.

The time arranged for the opening of the school at Rocky Spring, or York Collegiate Institute, as it will henceforth be called, was the first of January, '56. Soon after returning from South Lowell I received an invitation by letter to visit Salem Church, Alamance County, with a view to forming a class in Elocution and Grammar. I went and lectured, and a class in each was formed for a period of sixteen days, for that was as long as I could possibly stay, but the teaching of this class was the cause of some twelve or fifteen students going to York Collegiate Institute. The night after I reached Olin, a snow commenced falling and continued falling nearly all the next day. One or two wagons had been sent to move us to York Collegiate, but the weather was too bad for the family to turn out. In some three or four days after, we set our for Y. C. I., through the snow. This, the winter of '55-'56, was the coldest that had been known for a number of years. The snow lay on the ground nearly all the winter, and frequently it was some fifteen or eighteen inches deep. But, notwithstanding this, the school opened remarkably well. Within a few days after the opening of the school there were some twenty or twenty-five boarders present. The first session there were some fifty students, and a more promising set of young men and boys seldom come together. The first commencement came off early in June; the annual address was delivered by Professor Hill of Iredell. The declamation of the young men was very fine; hence the influence in favor of the school appeared to be very strong. During the vacation I preached and lectured at Mount Pleasant Church, Chatham

County, and formed a large class, principally in Grammar. The teaching of this class made a strong impression in favor of the Y. C. I.

About the middle of the fall session of Y. C. I., I left the school in charge of Professors Edwards and R. W. York, and set out for the town of Newbern, to which place I had previously been invited. On my way thither I stopped at Kernersville to fill an appointment that had been made some weeks previous. While there I met with a very remarkable child, a little girl about three years old, the daughter of Mr. James Stockton. I was informed that when the appointment was announced that a blind preacher would preach there at a certain time, she manifested unusual interest in the blind preacher, and frequently asked, "When will he come." When I entered the church she asked her mother, with much emotion, "Is that the blind preacher?" I was entertained during my stay by Mr. Stockton, the father of the child. She seemed almost to forget her father and mother while I remained, in her attention and devotion to me, manifesting the strongest possible affection. Some two years after, I stopped at Kernersville again, a protracted meeting having just commenced. After I had preached, as soon as I left the pulpit Brother Stockton met me and manifested much joy. As soon as our compliments had passed, I asked, "Where is Mary?" (I think that was her name). "Oh!" said he, "she has gone home." Notwithstanding his utterance seemed somewhat obstructed by emotion, I thought he meant that she was only gone home, as the house was a little out of town; but he meant that she had gone to her heavenly home. He said, moreover, that Mary never forgot the blind preacher, and frequently spoke of me with some emotion, and almost the last word she uttered was, "I am going home to heaven, and I expect to meet the blind preacher there."

On my way to Newbern I preached and lectured at Mount Pleasant Church, where I had taught a class, and another class was formed for twenty days, and while I was here, I was called upon to preach the funeral sermon of Sister Norwood. I preached from the text, "For we know that if this earthly house of our tabernacle were dissolved, we have a building of God, a house not made with hands, eternal in the heavens;" II Cor., 2 chap., 1 verse. The congregation was large, and the feeling intense.

After I had taught the class spoken of above, I set out in company with a young man by the name of Snipes, for Newbern. We took the train at Durham, and went to Goldsboro, and there we took the stage for Newbern, and reaching the place on Friday evening, stopped at the Washington House. My arrival was soon known. Not a few called on me, and several made donations. On Sunday I preached at the Methodist church to a large congregation, much interest being manifested. On Monday night I lectured to a large congregation assembled at the theatre. At the close of the lecture I was earnestly solicited to lecture again on the following night. I simply stated to the audience the object of my business, that I had came to form grammar classes, or any others they might desire. While at breakfast next morning, I was informed that a number of ladies had assembled in the parlor, desiring to see me. Soon as breakfast was over, I was introduced by Mr. Bryant, the proprietor of the hotel to some twelve or fifteen ladies, some married and some single, one of whom was Mrs. Green, wife of lawyer Green. They told me that they had come to take lessons in grammar, and wished to begin immediately. I furnished them with books, and commenced teaching forthwith. Mr. Bryant permitted us to teach in his parlor. This class continued to increase until it numbered some twenty-five. Another large class was formed in Mr. Mayhew's Academy; an Elocution class was formed at the parsonage. I met the class in the Washington House twice a day, giving them a morning and an evening lesson. The Elocution class was met a little before 11 a. m. Professor Mayhew and daughter were both members of the night class; his daughter is now Mrs. Hendren. I now had enough to keep myself and Mr. Snipes both busy. Mr. Bryant was a very liberal, clever man. He furnished a room to teach in, and coal to warm it, and boarded me and Mr. Snipes, and charged nothing but the tuition of two scholars. I continued teaching here some seven or eight weeks, and when I was ready to leave the ladies requested me to deliver a lecture in the theatre the night before I left, made me a concert, and notwithstanding there was a snow several inches deep on the ground, they raised between 80 and 90 dollars for my benefit. Than these a nobler set of ladies I have never met. While here I did what few Protestant ministers ever did--I baptised a child of a Catholic lady. Mr. Snipes continued teaching after I had left. Two young men accompanied me to Y. C. I. as students. The spring session of '57 had commenced before I reached home. Besides the donation, my tuition fees, and what the ladies raised at the concert, the members of the church where I had preached frequently took up a collection, and raised $24.00. The school at Y. C. I. was still in a flourishing condition, and continued so until sometime in '58, [when] I resigned. After my resignation, Professor Marler took charge of the school and continued for some three sessions. After he left Rev. T. L. Troy established a female school in the seminary--but thinly attended. During the war the house was badly damaged; no school, except I taught two or three grammar classes. After the war had closed, Colonel Flowers and myself opened a school in the house, and had a good school, considering the times. At the end of the first session he resigned, and I continued a session or two longer. After I had quit, Mr. Raymer and Colonel Flowers taught two sessions, and this was about the last teaching that was ever done in that house. The house was a gravel wall, and was miserably slighted in the building. It finally fell, or came near it, and has been removed for several years past.

During the interim between my resignation and the war my time was almost wholly occupied in traveling and lecturing and teaching and preaching. In the spring of '58 I went on a preaching tour, accompanied by Mr. Alfred Smith as a traveling companion. I delivered a series of sermons in Charlotte, which excited some interest. From there we went to Concord, and there I preached for some eight or ten days. At the first or second sermon, a revival broke out, which resulted in several converts. The church was also much revived and I was remunerated with some twenty-five or thirty dollars. I also preached at Thomasville, High Point, and Greensboro, though I made but a short stay at each of these places, but generally received some donations everywhere. I also preached in Raleigh at both stations, was kindly received, and handsomely remunerated. I spent a few days in Goldsboro, and then we went directly to Wilmington. There I remained some twelve days, preaching every night, and Sunday twice or three times. I alternated between the two stations; the congregations were large and a good deal of interest was manifested at both stations. The donations amounted to about $50.00. While I was preaching at Wilmington, I received a letter from Chapel Hill, inviting me to come there, and deliver a course of lectures; but I spent so much time in Wilmington, Goldsboro and Raleigh that I reached Chapel Hill too late for the lectures, as the faculty had already commenced examining the classes, immediately before the commencement. Notwithstanding my health was very bad, yet I preached several times in Chapel Hill. Dr. Jones, an eminent physician, who manifested much interest in my behalf, advised me to go home immediately and rest, as I was threatened with dropsy; but I went to Hillsboro and continued preaching there nearly a week. From there I went to South Lowell and preached, and then returned home, my health continuing bad. I remained at home some six or seven weeks,. My health having somewhat recovered, I set out from home with a view of teaching classes. We formed a class in Newbern in both English and French. We then went to

Kinston, and I delivered a seriees of lectures on one subject, The secret of success disclosed, for which I received some thirty or forty dollars. Then a class was formed in English Grammar, and also Watson formed a class in French. While we were teaching these classes the annual session of the North Carolina Conference came off at Newbern. We both attended the Conference. Bishop Kavanaugh presided. The members of the Conference generally manifested a great deal of interest in my enterprise, the publication of the High School Grammar, and Dr. Deems made a speech in my behalf before the Conference, urging the preachers to give me all the aid possible, especially by their influence. Conference having closed we returned to Kinston to wind up our classes. But before we left, through the influence of Dr. Deems, we both received free tickets on our way home. In some two or three days we wound up our affairs at Kinston, and set out for home. We changed cars at Goldsboro, but before we reacheed Greensboro we were informed that the train we were on did not connect with the train running from Salisbury to Statesville. Consequently we got off the train at Greensboro and waited for the train on the morrow; but just before we reached the depot the next day the train moved off, leaving us and perhaps fifty other passengers. At this I felt much chagrined as I had been from home three months, and was anxious to be there on Christmas. But after reflecting, it occurred to me that there might be a Providence in it, and I grieved no more about it. Mr. Michael Sherwood, a cousin of my first wife, took me from the hotel to his home where I was treated very kindly. Watson left on the night train. Dr. Burkhead, who was the stationed preacher, learning that I was left, called on me and asked me to preach for him next day (Sunday). I preached at the appointed hour, and received from some one a donation of $10.00, so it turned out for the best. Brother Thomas was to preach at night in Greensboro, but was rained out. The next day, however, was a pleasant day. I left on the train at two o'clock, p. m., reached Statesville in safety about dark, where I was met by Mrs. York and one of the little boys, and on the following day reached home, but remained no longer than we could make preparation for leaving again.

Early in January, '59, Mrs. York and myself set out with a view to travel principally in the eastern portion of the State. The special object we had in view was to raise funds to stereotype the High School Grammar. The first place we stopped at was Lexington. We continued there some two days. I preached twice, and lectured once, but did but little more than pay our board. We next stopped at High Point, where Mr. Langdon was conducting a female

Seminary. I lectured in the chapel of the Seminary. Notwithstanding the lecture was eulogized, the collection was very poor--the prospect so far was not flattering. We stopped at Raleigh, and received much enrouragement from Brother Bruton and other leading members of the church, but it was not thought to be a propitious time for a lecture. We then took the Raleigh & Gaston Road, and stopped at Henderson, Granville County, and there spent some four days, preaching and lecturing, and succeeded better here than we had done, but the result was not encouraging, but [we] were urged to stop on our return and preach. We next went to Warrenton and stopped at the hotel but in an hour or two we were taken to the parsonage by Brother Barrett, the P. C. Our stay here was very agreeable. I preached three times and lectured once, and the collection was far better than it was at any place we had previously visited, for we received between twenty and thirty dollars. We returned to Henderson and stopped with Brother Holmes, a superannuated preacher of the Virginia Conference, and next day being the Sabbath, I preached twice. While at church our valise was cut open, and something over $20 stolen, twice as much as we had collected at the place. We left Henderson and went to Franklinton. Here I remained, preaching and lecturing until the following Monday, and succeeded well. The success was principally owing to the interest manifested by Brother Maynard, a superannuated pracher. On Tuesday Brother Maynard took me to Louisburg, where I spent some three or four days preaching and lecturing--was kindly received, and well remunerated. We returned to Franklinton the next day and set out for Raleigh. We only stopped in Raleigh a few hours to wait for the train bound for Goldsboro, but during the time I delivered an address to the young ladies at Professor Bruton's Seminary.

We got off the train at Smithfield depot, took a hack for the town of Smithfield about four miles distant. It was after night when we arrived, and we put up at the hotel. The next morning Dr. Beckwith and other leading members of the church called on us, and we were taken to Dr. Beckwith's residence. At night I preached, and continued preaching for nearly a week to full congregations. There was much interest manifested, and the collection liberal. We then left for Goldsboro, and stopped at the Baker house, but the next day the Rev. S. Milton Frost, D. D., took us to the Wayne Female College, of which he was President. The following Sunday, which was next day, there was an appointment at 11 o'clock for Rev. C. P. Jones, Bible agent. He, however, generously offered to surrender his appointmnt, but I did not accept the offer, as I was unwell, and had been so ever since our arrival. The colored people had sent in a request for me to preach for them; the appointment was made, and also one for the night. At three o'clock the benches below were occupied by the colored people, and the gallery filled with white people. At night the white pople occupied the seats below, and the colored people the gallery. The house was packed to its utmost capacity, and I preached from the text: "Turn you to the strongholds, ye prisoners of hope." The effect was overwhelming and before I had closed the sermon, my voice was drowned by the crying and shouting of the people, both below and in the gallery. Brother Jones concluded, but his words were not "like apples of gold in pictures of silver," he severely reproved the colored people for the noise they had made and interrupting the preacher, when the white congregation was equally noisy. His remarks threw a chill over the whole congregation, and though he did not mention the white people, yet they felt it as a reproof, and as soon as we came out of the pulpit one of the leading members of the church said, "Brother Jones, why did you make any discrimination, for if there was any guilt about it we were equally as guilty as the colored people." The truth is, Brother Jones' remarks were universally condemned. I continued preaching there for something over a week to large congregations, but the gallery was almost deserted by the colored people. The truth is, they never got over the shock while I remained. I was, however, liberally rewarded.

We left on Monday for Wilson. We stayed at Wilson some four days. I preached three times in the church and delivered a lecture in Dr. Deems' Academy. I promised on my return to stop and preach again. Having wound up here, we took the hack for Greenville, and there went aboard the steamer Postboy for Washington which place we reached about 11 o'clock on Saturday. Arrangements had been made for us to board at the hotel as that was convenient to the church. Soon after dinner Brother Pell, P. C., called on us, and arrangements were made for me to preach at 11 o'clock next day. A large congregation had assembled, both white and colored, and much interest was manifested during the sermon, so much so that Brother Pell remarked to me, "Were your case presented to the congregation it would be an easy matter to raise $500.00 or $600.00. But," said he, "you will get enough anyhow." I preached again at night, and when I entered the house I found it no easy matter to reach the pulpit; for every aisle was filled with people on chairs. They also stood round the windows, and it was said that many left for want of accommodation. I continued there four or five days, preaching every night but one, when it rained all night The last night I preached the effect was very fine. Though no effort was made by the preacher to take up a collection, we received between one hundred and two hundred dollars, and as much goods as we could carry. While here I received a letter inviting me to Greenville. The night before I left Washington I had the Asthma extremely bad, and we had to be at the wharf before light. The Asthma was so severe that I had to be carried aboard the steamer, but had not been there more than ten or fifteen minutes before I was perfectly relieved. A similar thing occurred in leaving Hyde afterwards, nor did I ever suffer with Asthma while traveling by water. We reached Greenville Thursday morning at 10 o'clock, and were conducted to the house of the Hon. Mr. Hoyt. We were kindly received by Mrs. Hoyt, and were hospitably entertained during our stay in Greenville, he not being at home. I preached at this place about a week, but as Mrs. York was taken sick, we were detained nearly two weeks. We were liberally remunerated for what preaching I did and as soon as Mrs. York was able to travel we took the stage for Wilson, where I was expected to preach, but was too sick to do it, but the people sent in a liberal donation. On the next day we took the train for Goldsboro, but made no tarrying, but took the train on the A. R. R.

* Evidently the Atlantic and North Carolina Railroad. [Ed.]

An appointment was outstanding in Craven County for Sunday. On reaching the depot where we had to leave, we found no one there to meet us, but there was a Baptist preacher aboard who had an appointment in the country for the next day. He was met by a gentleman, and they very kindly offered us the buggy while they took it afoot. We stopped at Brother White's, a member of the church living near where I was to preach the next day. We were kindly received, and found ourselves, weary as we were, pleasantly domiciled with a good family. We also met with the P. C. of the Craven Circuit, who informed me that the arrangements were all made for me to preach next day at 11 o'clock. The morning dawned, but the sky was overcast with dark murky clouds, and the rain was fast falling, which continued until about 4 o'clock in the evening; consequently I did not preach. Soon after the rain ceased.

AT WASHINGTON, N. C.--1860 AND 1861.

The winter '60 and '61 was spent at this place. I reached here, traveling alone, the last of November and preached on Sunday and lectured on Monday night; but the weather was so inclement, the night being rainy, cold and dark, that but few attended. A small class, however, in Logic and Grammar was formed. This session of twenty days terminated just before Christmas. Other classes were formed, though not large. I then returned and spent the Christmas holidays at home. Early in January following, I set out with William, my son, then a little boy, for Washington, to meet a previous engagement. Soon after reaching the place I began teaching night and day, and generally preached twice on Sunday.

A MYSTERIOUS PROVIDENCE.

Just before this session closed I was taken sick and was scarcely able to finish. I was so very sick that Doctors Tayloe and Ruffin were called in. For two weeks or more I suffered intensely, and, as I was paying high board, this appeared to be against me. In this, however, I was mistaken, as the sequel shows. While sick, Dr. Tayloe became acquainted with York's High School Grammar, New York edition, having purchased a copy and after having examined it, he said it surpassed anything he had ever seen on the subject of Grammar, both as to matter and arrangement. Consequently he, together with several others, requested me to deliver a public lecture as soon as able. To this I consented. The time was appointed to lecture in the Court House on a certain night. Having been thoroughly published, the house was packed to its utmost capacity. The lecture was popular. After it was closed Charles P. Jones, P. C., Professor Richardson and Dr. Tayloe made several complimentary remarks, urging the people to embrace the opportunity to acquire a knowledge of the English language, after which many joined the classes who had not been in before, and classes were formed in various places on Grammar and Logic. A class of ladies was formed in Judge Warren's hall room. The several classes now amounted to about $20.00 per day, so that my sickness proved to be a blessing. I continued teaching until the first of March, and at the close my prospects were never so bright for success, as I was invited to various places, and urged to return to Washington early in May. In the meantime, however, the war cloud was gathering thick and dark, and its portentious thunder proclaimed its speedy approach. On my return home I called on my publisher, Mr. Pomeroy, in the city of Raleigh, and urged him to send without delay for the stereotyped plates in New York, as I believed that war was inevitable. This he promised to do, but put off sending too long, consequently the plates were lost, which was a serious loss to me.

CHAPTER XII.

THE COMMENCEMENT OF THE WAR.

About the middle of April I set out to meet my first engagement at Morehead City. On reaching Salisbury, as I recollect on the 15th of April, I found society thoroughly stirred from center to circumference; for President Lincoln's proclamation calling for 75,000 soldiers had reached there. Now the brilliancy of my prospects was obscured; nothing but a dark unknown presented itself. We, for Willie was with me, went on to meet the engagement, but found it difficult to get a seat in any car, as every car was literally crowded with soldiers. On reaching the City we found that the desire for Grammar had passed away, and was supplanted by that of war; for regiment after regiment of soldiers was passing, as the city was in the immediate vicinity of Fort Macon. Dr. Yates was then stationed at Morehead City as P. C. I preached in his church twice on Sunday, and on the following days delivered a series of lectures consisting of four on one subject, "The Secret of Success Disclosed." They were well attended, and reasonably remunerated. The lectures having closed, we left for home, but on our way called at Lenoir Institute, where I taught a class in Punctuation. Seeing no other opening, we returned home. Soon after reaching there I was taken sick, which resulted in Typhoid fever, consequently I was confined for several weeks.

HOW I STOOD TOWARDS THE WAR.

I was opposed to secession, because I believed that secession and war were synonyms, or meant the same thing. Nor was I ever a stickler for the institution of slavery, for if the institution were not wrong, per se, yet it was the cause of many and enormous sins. I also believed that those who had the least interest in slavery would have to face the danger and make the greatest sacrifice of health and life. But after the War was fully inaugurated and inevitably, my sympathies were with the South, though I could see but a faint prospect of success, for it appeared to me that nothing but the favor of Divine Providence could lead to her success; and for that favor we had but little hope, for the leaders were moved by ambition and hatred.

After I had recovered from the fever I attended a camp-meeting which was then called Upper Pisgah, then on the Alexander Circuit, during which time I was soliciteed to teach a Grammar Class in that neighborhood. After some two or three weeks had elapsed, I returned and delivered a lecture, and a class was formed, principally of young ladies. It continued forty days, and closed near Christmas. I have no recollection of engaging in anything else during that winter.

SECOND YEAR OF THE WAR, '62.

During the early part of the year I did but little for every avenue to teaching was nearly closed. I only taught a very small class at home, and preached generally on Sunday. In the latter part of the summer I was invited to attend a camp-meeting held by the Protestant Methodists, located in the neighborhood of Marion. I set out alone to attend it and others. I stopped at Morganton and preached twice on Sunday. At the close of the first sermon a gentleman of Virginia presented me with a twenty dollar bill. This came at an opportune time, for my purse was almost empty. I was earnestly requested to continue longer, but my health did not appear to justify it. So, on the following Monday evening, I secured a seat in the stage hack for Marion, and reached that place about 11 o'clock p. m. I was met and kindly received by Dr. Abernethy, who was running a school at that place. On Thursday night I preached in the Court House to a full congregation, and lectured on Friday night in the Seminary. On Saturday I was conveyed to the camp-meeting by Dr. Abernethy. During the meeting I preached five times. The meeting was a success and I received in donations some thirty dollars. During the meeting two men came from Cleveland County to take me to a camp-meeting to be held in that county at a church called Clover Hill. On my return to Marion I found a number of ladies assembled at Dr. Abernethy's, who presented me with two pairs of pants, a vest and some other articles of clothing. This was a God-send, as my wardrobe had become very scanty. On the next day we set out for the camp-meeting in Cleveland, passing over some roads so bad that a man had to walk on each side of the buggy to keep it from upsetting. We reached Colonel Peeler's late in the evening, with whom I spent the night. I was kindly received and hospitably entertained, which was quite refreshing, as I was both weary and sick. On Saturday the Colonel took me to the Camp-meeting, where I was gladly received by the P. C. and the public generally. Though unwell, I preached every day of the meeting, and on Sunday at 11 o'clock there was an unusual move on the congregation. The P. C. received a number into the church. I received a donation of some $30 or $40. At the close of the meeting a man was there for me to go to another camp-meeting to be held in Gaston County. I went and preached twice on the road, receiving donations at each place. We reached the campground on Friday evening. I was cordially received by the P. C. and the people. I preached each day of the meeting, and the Lord was present to work. From that point I was taken to Newton, where I continued three days, but was so unwell that I preached only one sermon. On Friday morning I went aboard the train with a view to attending another camp-meeting to be held at Nebo, in McDowell County, to which I had been invited before leaving Marion. At this meeting I not only preached each day, but on two days I preached twice. Sunday, though feeble, I preached in the morning and at night. There was considerable work during the meeting, and not a few were added to the church, the precise number not recollected. I received at this meeting some $70 in donations. On Sunday night I was taken sick, supposed to have been caused by excessive work and exposure. Be that as it may, it was with much difficulty that I reached home, and I was for several weeks confined to my bed. With this tour terminated my labors, principally, for this year.

CHAPTER XIII.

THIRD YEAR OF THE WAR--63.

During the early part of this year I did but little except teaching a small grammar class and preaching on Sunday. In the latter part of July I left home for another preaching tour, though my health was far from being good, and, as I had no traveling companion the prospect appeared gloomy; but necessity pressed me onward. I went aboard the train at Statesville for Camp Vance and preached several times to the soldiers. They appeared to be grateful for the service rendered, and manifested it by a liberal donation, though Confederate money at this time had so depreciated that it was worth but little. From there I went to Morganton, where I met Brother Watts, P. C., of the Morganton Circuit, who informed me that he had just commenced a protracted meeting in the neighborhood. He urged me to go out with him, to which I readily consented as I had no appointments beyond. I remained some three days preaching at this meeting, but on the last day but one, I was taken quite sick, and was taken back to Morganton, and Dr. Happole was called in. For several days I was treated by him, being domiciled in the parsonage. As soon as I was able to travel, I set out with Brother Watts, and preached at various places on his work. The preaching at Gilboa Church had a good effect. A Confederate soldier present was deeply impressed and took up a collection without mentioning it to the P. C. Brother Watts appointed a protracted meeting to begin at that place four weeks hence, and I was strongly urged to attend. From this place we went to Snow Hill, near Mr. Rutherford's. Here I was met by Marcus Kaylor, a local Methodist preacher, who took me to Brother Gardener's, his father-in-law. There was an appointment outstanding at a church nearby on the following Thursday. The special object of the meeting was to pray for the soldiers and the success of the Confederate Arms. Many people were out. By request I preached to them. The sermon had a fine effect on the audience, and several presented themselves at the altar as penitents. The meeting was protracted, and I continued preaching every day, and frequently twice a day for some ten days. It resulted in much good. Brothers Kaylor, England, and some others aided in the meeting. The camp-meeting at Nebo was now approaching and I was importuned to attend it. While resting a few days previous to the meeting I visited Marion and preached a number of times there. The time for the meeting having arrived, Brother Kaylor took me to it. I remained until its close, preaching on each day. The meeting was a success. Not a few professed faith in Christ, the number not remembered. After it had closed I went to Gilboa Church to attend the protracted meeting. I preached on Friday, and was taken sick soon after. I was kindly entertained by John Dorsey, a local Methodist preacher, but notwithstanding I was sick, I preached on Saturday and Sunday. On Sunday the prospect was exceedingly fine. Perhaps as many as twenty or twenty-five penitents were at the altar. I was too sick to continue longer at the meeting and it was continued by some of the local brethren. Brother Watts took me that afternoon to Morganton. It was my intention to take the train next day and go home, but I found myself on Monday morning not able to sit up. Dr. Happole was again called in, and I was subjected to a course of medicine. For several days I was confined in the Parsonage, but never could anyone be more kindly treated, especially by Sister Watts, who lingered by my bedside as a guardian angel, and seemed to anticipate every want. As soon as I was able to travel I left for home. On reaching there I found a protracted meeting begun by Brother Parker, P. C., and Brother Stevenson, a local preacher from Tennessee. Though quite feeble I preached on Sunday. During the meeting many were added to the church, and the members were greatly revived.

    While at the camp-meeting at Nebo, a gentleman by the name of Greenlee, who was confined at home by sickness, requested me through his wife to come and preach in his house, as he was very desirous to hear me, and if I could not come directly from the meeting to come as soon as convenient. I could not go then as I had promised to attend the protracted meeting at Gilboa Church, but intended to visit him as soon as this meeting should close, but sickness prevented me. Consequently I went home, but as soon as I was able to travel and preach, I set out with a view to attending to his request, preaching at various places on the way. But on reaching Esq. Murphy's, three miles from Marion, I learned that Mr. Greenlee was dead. I continued there some three or four days, praching in a church nearby by the name of Murphy's Chapel. Mr. Murphy was a kind, liberal man, but he was not a Christian. His wife, however, was a devoted Christian, and a member of the M. E. Church, South. From this place I went to the Widow Greenlee's who received me cordially and treated me with no little kindness. Here I met with a daughter of General Jackson, of Tennessee, who was a refugee from that State. She was a lady of intelligence and agreeable manners. On Sunday following I went to Marion and preached twice, and then left for Rutherford College. After reaching there, I preached some three or four nights in succession. The people were attentive, and appeared to be much impresseed.

Mr. Hayes, the father-in-law of Dr. Abrnethy, was present, and as he left for home Sunday afternoon, I took a seat in the buggy with him, and on the next day I was sent to Esq. Marshal's, and on the day following I was sent to Taylorsville, and from there home. I reached there only a few days before my youngest son, Davidson Victor, was born. His birthday was the 24th of November, 1863.

During this and the year next preceding, I assisted the preacher in charge on the Alexander Circuit in holding several meetings, viz.: Upper Pisgah, Liberty, Stony Point, and Hopewell. At these meetings much good was accomplished.

CHAPTER XIV.

FOURTH YEAR OF THE WAR.

During the winter of '63-'64 I taught several Grammar Classes at York Collegiate Institute, and preached on Sunday when able. As soon as warm weather returned I was invited to make another preaching tour in the western portion of the State, but the night before I was to set out I was taken very sick, which sickness continued several weeks; consequently I was prevented from making the tour. As soon as I was able to preach, Brother R. T. M. Stephenson and myself held a protracted meeting at New Schoolhouse, during which we have reason to believe good was accomplished. I also assisted Brother M. V. Sherrill in holding a meeting at Hopewell, which resulted in the conversion of several, and also several accessions to the church. On the first of October I was sent for to go to Low Pisgah to help carry on a meeting which had been commenced by some other preachers who had left the meeting. I went, and the first sermon I preached was on Thursday night. During this service there were some two or three converts. I continued at night only until Sunday night, with more or less success each night. I preached twice on Sunday. On Sunday night we had twenty-one converts and scarcely was there a sinner who was not a penitent. As well as I recollect, the same number joined the church.

During this year it was my sad duty to preach the funeral sermon of several Confederate soldiers. The War was now hastening to a close. On the following April, General Lee surrendered, which was virtually the end of the War. During those dark days of War, Mrs. York remained at home, and with some small boys, cultivated a small farm, the products of which were the principal support of the family. Not only so, but the family was clothed by her untiring industry, nor did she ever murmur or complain of her hard lot. And last, but not least, she was untiring in waiting on me when sick.

CHAPTER XV.
1865.

THE END OF THE WAR. UNSETTLED STATE OF SOCIETY AND SCARCENESS OF PROVISIONS.--SCHOOL TAUGHT AT YORK COLLEGIATE INSTITUTE--TWO SONS IN THE WAR.

The War was now ended, leaving society in an unsettled and almost lawless condition. Soldiers were returning home. Deserters were coming out of their lurking places and robbers in many places were prowling about like hungry wolves. Provisions were exceedingly scarce. The people were almost without a currency, but gradually law and order were restored and schools began to spring up. During this year I taught two sessions at York Collegiate Institute. Col. [G. W.] Flowers was associated with me as teacher during the first session. Considering the times the school was well attended, but to pay in money was almost impossible. By the income of the school and the products of the little farm, my family was supported. During the year I preached at various places, and aided the P. C. in several protracted meetings, and some two camp-meetings. I had two sons in the War. R. W. York went from Wake County as Captain of Company I of the 6th Regiment; afterwards he was promoted, and was Major of the same regiment during the War. In the latter part of the War he was wounded, and did but little more active service. My other son, W. C. York, belonged to what was called the Junior Reserves, and was lieutenant of the company to which he belonged. He returned home unhurt.

CHAPTER XVI.
1866.

TRAVELING AND LECTURING AND TEACHING CLASSES--AT SNOW CREEK CAMP MEETING AND SUNDAY-SCHOOL CONVENTION AT ROCK SPRING.

Early in this year I commenced traveling, having a young man by the name of Blankenship as my traveling companion. The scene of our travels was various, but the most of our time was spent in the southern portion of Iredell County. During this time I taught Grammar and Arithmetic classes. Classes were formed at McKendrie's Chapel, Wesley's Chapel, and other places, names not recollected. I delivered public lectures in various places and preached frequently, generally twice on the Sabbath.

Towards the latter part of the year Mr. Blankenship and I dissolved partnership. After he left I taught classes in Lincoln and Catawba counties. Though traveling alone for the most part, I got along well and succeeded well. During this year I attended a camp-meeting at Snow Creek, and also attended a Sunday School Convention at Rock Spring Camp-ground, which continued several days. Various addresses were delivered by different men, and four sermons were preached on Sunday. This was the most interesting Sunday school celebration it has ever been my pleasure to attend Some six or eight schools were present, and were examined by their superintendents respectively.

CHAPTER XVII.

CLASSES TAUGHT AT CATAWBA STATION--THREE CAMP MEETINGS VISITED--
A PREACHING AND VISITING TOUR--PREACHING AT VARIOUS PLACES--
MEETING WITH MANY BRETHREN AND SISTERS FOR THE LAST TIME.

Early in the year '67 I taught a class in Grammar and Arithmetic at Catawba Station, which continued forty days. At the close of the class I was taken quite sick, but preached on the way home. After my health was restored I attended and preached at three camp-meetings in succession, viz.: Snow Creek, Rock Springs, and Sharon. At each of these meetings Rev. Thos. G. Lowe was present and preached, though then in feeble health. I hardly ever heard his equal as a pulpit orator, but life was fast ebbing out, and in a few months he died. In September of this year, Mrs. York and I set out to visit relatives and friends in Randolph and Guilford. On our way I lectured and preached at Mocksville and also visited a school in the vicinity, and at the request of the teacher, lectured to the students. At Thomasville, at the request of the president, Rev. D. R. Bruton, I lectured to the young ladies of Thomasville Female Seminary. We spent a few hours at Trinity College, where I met with Rev. Peter Doub, D. D., for the last time. His health was then feeble, and in two or three years after he passed away. We reached Union Factory, now Randleman, just at the time the Methodist Protestants were commencing a protracted meeting. At the request of many we promised to return on Sunday morning to aid in the meeting. On Saturday I preached at Cool Springs Church, a church to which I used to resort in my boyhood days. Here I met with Brother Charley Philips, that good and useful man who has since passed to his reward. On Sunday morning following we returned to Union, and preached twice that day, and also on Monday and Tuesday, and good doubtless was done. On Wednesday I went to fill an appointment outstanding at Gray's Chapel. Here I met with many of my old friends from different neighborhoods. The meeting was a feast of love and joy. Since then nearly all of those dear brethren and sisters with whom I used to associate and to whom I used to preach have gone to their reward. On the day following we returned to Union to meet an appointment on Thursday night which had been made. We found there a very large congregation assembled. After the church had been packed to its utmost capacity, it was believed that scarcely half of the people had entered. On the Saturday following I preached at Level Cross to a full congregation, and on Sunday morning at Rehoboth, about six miles south of Greensboro. The crowd was large and the effect tremendous. Here I was requested by Brother Westbrooks to preach at

Greensboro. In the afternoon I preached at Red Hill Church of the M. P. Church. The effect was good, and I was urged to hold a protracted meeting at this place. To this I consented. The appointment was made for it to commence on Thursday following. On Monday we went to Greensboro. I preached on Monday night to a full house, and several penitents were at the altar. On Tuesday night I preached again, perhaps to a larger congregation. Some three or four professed faith in Christ. On Wednesday we returned to the neighborhood of Red Hill, and on Thursday began preaching, according to appointment, assisted by Rev. Samuel Lineberry, brother of Mrs. York, and Brother Gambol, a zealous and efficient exhorter of the Methodist Episcopal Church, South. It continued until Sunday without apparently accomplishing much good, but on Sunday I preached twice, and the Word took effect, and on Sunday night there were perhaps some twelve or fifteen penitents, and several converts. We held meeting on Monday and Tuesday nights, and the work continued to increase, and Tuesday night, as well as I recollect, there were some eight or ten converts. The meeting was now left in the hands of others. Wednesday after dinner we set out for home. We reached Turnersburg on Saturday and stopped with Brother Wilford Turner, and were kindly received. Then we learned that a camp-meeting had just begun at Harmony Hill, a union campground some seven miles distant. We were so strongly urged to attend it, that though we had been from home so long, yet we consented to go. I preached on Saturday night and twice on Sunday. On Monday morning we left for home and reached there that day, and found all well.

CHAPTER XVIII.

LOGIC CLASSES TAUGHT AT STATESVILLE--A CLASS FORMED AT OLIN HIGH SCHOOL, ONE IN SALISBURY--PREACHED IN THREE DIFFERENT PLACES--POLITICAL EXCITEMENT--COLORED CHURCHES--GRAMMAR CLASSES TAUGHT IN STATESVILLE--A VISIT TO MAJOR YORK'S--GRAMMAR CLASSES TAUGHT IN CHATHAM AND WAKE--RUFFIN BADGER INSTITUTE.

Soon after reaching home as stated in a former chapter, I was employed by some preachers to go to Statesville to teach them Logic, as a preparation for an examination at the approaching conference. While there I was invited by Prof. R. L. Abernethy to visit Rutherford College; but before I was through with the course on instruction I was taken very sick, and Dr. Douthet, who had been a student of mine at Clemonsville High School, was immediately called in. For several days I was treated by him, who gave me the closest possible attention. Soon after I had recovered I went to Olin High School and preached on Sunday and Sunday night, and lectured on Monday night. A class in Grammar and Arithmetic was formed. I commenced teaching about the 1st of December. I continued there during the winter of '67 and '68, and wound up the first of April. Before leaving there I received a letter inviting me to Salisbury. About the middle of April I visited that place. I delivered a public lecture there, and formed a class in Grammar and Logic. The Grammar was instructed in the day and the Logic at night. Rev. Dr. Rumple, pastor of the Presbyterian Church, Rev. C. Plyler, pastor of the M. E. Church, South, and Captain Wharton, principal of the Salisbury High School, were members of the Logic class. I continued teaching there until sometime in June. While there I generally preached twice on Sunday, principally in the M. E. Church, South, but occasionally in the Presbyterian and in the afternoon in the Court House to the negro congregation. But whites as well as blacks were listeners.

There were a great many colored people in town at this time, and three churches had been erected by them, or rather for them, viz.: Baptist, Presbyterian, and Methodist. But the Methodist, either by accident or incendiary, had just been burned, hence the reason of their holding their services in the Court House. The Baptist colored people used their house both as a church and as a school-room. As a school-room it was well furnished with maps, charts and other apparatus. Two well-educated ladies from the North taught the school, but because they taught the colored people the people of Salisbury did not associate with them, hence they were seldom seen at church, except the colored. They were efficient, industrious teachers, instructing the children by day and the adults by night. This was a time of great political excitement. The new Constitution was before the people to be received or rejected. The Democrats opposed and the Republicans were in favor of it. Scarcely a week passed while I was there but a political meeting of some kind was convened in the town hall. Many speeches were delivered pro and con, but when the election came on the new Constitution was adopted.

As I passed through Statesville on my return home I was strongly solicited to teach a class in that place. After a few days' rest at home I visited Statesville, delivered a public lecture and formed a class both for day and night. Dr. E. A. Yates was then pastor of the church. About the time I began teaching one of his children died. In consequence, his wife refused to stay longer, hence they both went to Beaufort, and he returned no more as pastor, and I filled his place while teaching the class. A quarterly meeting that had been appointed for that place was neither attended by presiding elder nor preacher in charge, presiding elder being sick. Hence I had all the preaching to do.

In a few days after the closing of this class Mrs. York and myself set out for Chatham County, with a view to visiting our son, Major York, whom we had not seen since the War. We reached there on Saturday, the 19th day of July, '68, and on the next day I preached at O'Kelly's Chapel in the morning and in the evening at Martha's Chapel. On the following day I preached at O'Kelley's Chapel by request, and also delivered a public lecture. On the following Wednesday I delivered a lecture at Martha's Chapel, and on the following Sunday preached at Mount Pisgah, in the Baptist church, and lectured on Monday. A large Grammar class was formed at this church. Scholars came from O'Kelly's and Martha's Chapel also. This class continued forty days, after which I taught a short session at Martha's Chapel. At its close I taught twenty days at Morrisville. At the close of this, another twenty days' class was taught in the vicinity of that place. During these several classes I was strongly solicited to establish a regular academical school at what was formerly called Northeast Academy. But as the house was removed from its former location, it was enlarged and improved. After the school had opened it was named Ruffin Badger Institute. As Christmas was now approaching, and the appointment having been made for opening the school at Ruffin Badger Institute early in January, we returned to spend Christmas holidays at home.

CHAPTER XIX.

RUFFIN BADGER INSTITUTE--EDUCATIONAL ASSOCIATION ORGANIZED--TEACHERS' MEETING FORMED--ELECTED PROFESSOR IN RUTHERFORD COLLEGE--PREPARING "MAN OF BUSINESS" FOR PUBLICATION--DEATH OF FANNIE S. YORK--ORGANIZATION OF LOCAL MINISTERS' CONFERENCE.

On the first of January, '69, the regular school organized at Ruffin Badger Institute was opened. It was well attended. Nearly forty were enrolled. I was assisted by Mr. Rufus Barbee and Miss Dell Moring; also Mrs. York regularly heard a Grammar class in the afternoon. During the session I preached at O'Kelly's Chapel, Mount Pisgah, Massey's Chapel, and occasionally at various other places.

A Literary Society was early organized and was well attended, not only by the students, but leading men of the neighborhood took an active part in the debates. At the close of the session the school was addressed by John Manning, Esq. Other gentlemen also made pertinent remarks and as far as I know the examination of the students gave entire satisfaction. During the first session the Chatham Educational Association was formed, and Maj. R. W. York was elected president. Its first meeting was held at Pittsboro. According to previous arrangement I delivered an address before the Association. Subject: "The English Language--the Importance of Its Study." The meeting was well attended, and very interesting, various subjects being discussed.

This Association continued in active operation for four years, holding its regular meetings, discussing various subjects on education, also having regular addresses delivered by educated gentlemen. Meetings were also held for the instruction of teachers, educated men being appointed to deliver lectures on various scientific subjects. The first teachers' meeting the following gentlemen were elected to deliver lectures to the teachers: Rev. Mr. Sutton on Geography; Captain Denson, on Mathematics; and myself on English Language and Elocution.

The school at Ruffin Badger continued in successful operation for four years. At the close of the spring session of '71 a silver-mounted cane was presented to me as a token of the appreciation of my services both in the pulpit and chair, by members of the Masonic Lodge, trustees, faculty and students of Ruffin Badger.

At the commencement of Rutherford College in May, 72, I was elected Professor of Belles-Lettres, embracing the English Language, Logic, Rhetoric and Elocution. At the close of the last session, Dec. 13, '72, I resigned as principal of Ruffin Badger, at which time a gold medal was presented to me by the patrons and students as an appreciation of the services rendered. Between the time of my resignation and my entering upon my professorship at Rutherford College, I was engaged in preparing "The Man of Business and Railroad Calculator" for publication, traveling, lecturing, and teaching classes. On the sixth of June, '71, my daughter Fannie, who had been for sometime assisting me in the school, died, and was buried at O'Kelly's Chapel, and her funeral sermon was preached by Rev. L. Branson, A. M., of Raleigh, on the 20th day of August. Her death was to me a bitter and protracted grief, for she had been for some years my eyes to see, and hand to write; but I have the best of reasons for believing that my loss was her eternal gain. She had been a member of the church from the age of 12, and her life was in every way consistent with her profession.

While principal of the Ruffin Badger Institute, the North Carolina Local Ministers' Conference was organized at Durham, N. C. I was elected President, and Rev. L. Branson, A. M., Secretary and Treasurer. Several local preachers were in attendance and preached on various subjects. This Conference has continued in successful operation, holding its annual meetings at various places ever since. The object of this conference is solely to increase the usefulness of its members and to extend the kingdom of Christ. Those ministers who criticised and frowned upon this organization must surely have been wholly ignorant of its true character.

CHAPTER XX.

LECTURING TOUR, VISITING GRAHAM, N. C., SYLVIAN ACADEMY, MOUNT VERNON SPRINGS--RUTHERFORD COLLEGE COMMENCEMENT--CLASS TAUGHT AT COLUMBIA AND FRANKLINSVILLE FACTORIES--ASSUMES THE DUTIES OF PROFESSORSHIP AT RUTHERFORD COLLEGE.

In the spring of '72, while "The Man of Business" was passing through the press, I, accompanied by my son William, made a short lecturing tour. Visited, lectured and preached at Graham. We were cordially received and entertained by the professors, D. A. and W. S. Long, who were conducting a school of high grade at this place. I lectured some two or three times in the school building; and preached in the Christian Church on Sunday to a full congregation. We then visited Sylvian Academy, and were welcomed by Professor Thomson, who was running a school there. Notice being given to the neighborhood, I lectured to a large audience at 2 o'clock p. m. We then went to Mount Vernon Spring, in Chatham County. Captain Siler was then principal of a school at that place. I lectured at night on education, to a full house. By request of the Captain and others I lectured again at 9 o'clock A. M. We then returned home, and after one day's rest I visited the commencement at Rutherford College. It was there arranged for me to take position as professor at the opening of the fall session. Sometime in the month of June following, I set out with the view to go to Rutherford College by private conveyance, accompanied by my son William. I preached and lectured at Columbia Factory, and a Grammar Class was formed. I also preached and lectured at Franklinsville, and a class was formed there. We continued here some five weeks, as the classes were taught at night only, both at the same time by myself and William, alternating. While teaching these classes I preached on the Sabbath at several places, viz.: Columbia, Franklinsville, Gray's Chapel, and Cool Springs. At the close of these classes, Mrs. York and a part of the family having joined me, we went directly to Rutherford College, and entered upon my professorship on the first day of August, '73.

CHAPTER XXI.

BEGIN LABOR IN RUTHERFORD COLLEGE AS PROFESSOR AND AGENT--TEACHING SIDE CLASSES--NEW COLLEGE BUILDING ERECTED--LECTURING IN COLLEGE ON SOCIAL LAW AND ETIQUETTE--VISITING VARIOUS CAMP-MEETINGS--REVIVAL AMONG THE STUDENTS--RESIGNATION AS AGENT AND PROFESSOR.

At this time the faculty of Rutherford College consisted of three Professors, a Music teacher, and a Primary teacher. Rev. R. L. Abernethy. D. D., Professor of Moral and Mental Philosophy and Modern Languages; J. T. Abernethy, Professor of Greek and Latin Languages; and I, Professor of Belles-Lettres--embracing higher English, Logic, Rhetoric, and Elocution; Miss Emma Abernethy, Music teacher, and the Primary teacher. A short time after entering upon the duties of my profession I was elected Agent of the College by the Trustees, and for some two or three years performed a double work of teacher and agent. I also frequently taught side classes in Logic and Grammar, consequently my labors were severe. During the term of my agency, a new college building was erected, much larger and more commodious than the former one. The college was well attended by students. The number would average perhaps 150 per session. Each year, while in the College, I delivered at night a series of lectures on Social Law and Etiquette, frequently preached in the College, at Hickory, Morganton, and Lenoir, and visited and preached at various Camp-meetings, viz.: Rocky Creek, Nebo, Mount Pleasant, Bald's Creek, Liberty, Mount Pisgah and Rocky Springs.

I continued as professor in the college for nearly five years, commencing 1st August, '73, and resigning at the close of the fall session of '77. The college did and has done much toward educating the masses, for none were neglected because they had no means to pay. The President was unusually liberal, consequently he aided those that could not help themselves. He was prompt in the discharge of his duties as President, punctual to the hours of beginning and ending. He was an industrious and laborious teacher, pleasant and agreeable in his manners--in short, he has done much, very much for the cause of education. He is still President, laboring and teaching, though he is now growing old (March 24, 1888). He is also a popular preacher and successful lecturer. He is also untiring in the defense of Temperance and Prohibition.

Each year we had one and sometimes two revivals of religion in the College. During these revivals many professed faith in Christ. Many became ministers of the gospel, both traveling and local. At the close of the fall session of '77, as has already been stated, I resigned as professor, having sometime previous resigned as agent, though we still lived at the college until August, '81.

CHAPTER XXII.

LEAVING FOR ARKANSAS--ARRIVAL--DISAPPOINTMENT--LECTURING AND TEACHING CLASSES IN RUSSELLVILLE--AT DARDENELLE--AT ATHENS--LEWISBURG--CONWAY--LONE OAK--ARRIVAL AT HOME.

Some two months before I resigned my position with Rutherford College, I received a letter from Mr. Tillman Man of Russellville, Ark., a man with whom I had been acquainted in this State, stating that the Board of Education of Russellville had elected me principal of a High School at that place, with a salary of $1,200, to be paid partly from the public fund and partly from subscription. Mr. Man was not a member of the board, but wrote for the secretary, as he was acquainted with me. This correspondence was kept up until I resigned my position in the college. Having no doubt as to the truth of what was written, at the close of the fall session of '77 I resigned my position in that institution, and on the 29th day of January, '78, I and my son Bascom set out for Arkansas, and on 2nd day of February reached Russellville. On the following day, being Sunday, I preached in the M. E. Church, South. At the close of the sermon I announced that I would lecture on Monday night in the school building, called the college, and that I wished to meet the Board of Education at the earliest possible day, as we were present and wished to commence teaching at the earliest opportunity. My surprise may be imagined but never described when, after the benediction had been pronounced, the preacher in charge announced that Professor Doggette on Monday week would commence teaching in the college, according to a previous arrangement, which had only been made, as we learned afterwards, the day before. The Schoolhouse which they called the College, belonged to an individual of whom Professor Doggette had rented it. We now found ourselves in an awful predicament, being nearly 1,200 miles from home, and almost without any money, and excepting Mr. Man, among entire strangers. But according to appointment, I delivered the lecture on Monday night, and stated to the audience what had occurred. At the request of several gentlemen, I lectured again the next night, and a collection was taken up, and some eight or ten dollars were received. A Grammar Class was also formed, which was to be taught at night. As soon as the Board of Education met we met with them, and the correspondence between Mr. Man and myself was read, at which the President of the Board expressed his surprise, as no such action had ever been taken by the Board. The Secretary of the Board confessed, however, that he had authorized Mr. Mann to correspond with me and to make the statement already mentioned. But the reason of this procedure was still behind the curtain. The President of the Board stated that the salary promised was none too much, but they had neither the money nor a house.

During our stay at Russellville some ladies waited on me, and requested me to deliver a lecture on Love. I consented to do so, and the time and place was fixed upon. These ladies, who were five in number, without my knowledge had tickets printed which they sold for the lecture, and raised nearly $40 for the lecture, for whom the following verses were composed, and to whom they were dedicated and were published in some of the papers of the State:

AN APOSTROPHE TO WOMAN.

BY REV. B. YORK, D. D.

Woman, what magic in thy name!
Who hath not felt its power?
The best, the richest gift to man,
Earth's fairest, sweetest flower.

Yes, heaven's best earthly gift to man,
To him so kindly given,
With love to gild Life's narrow span,
And help him on to heaven.

The Muses' fondest wreath is thine:
Thy praise their tongues employ;
Through thickest gloom thy love doth shine
And all is bright with joy.

Without thy love, without thy smile,
How dark this world would be--
A world without a sun to shine,
Or ray of light to cheer!

Without thee, what is boasted home?
A dark and cheerless night;
But to that home thou art the sun
That cheers and makes it bright.

May joy and peace thy steps attend
Through life's eventful road;
And when thy useful work is done,
Thy spirit live with God.

(Russellville, Ark., Feb. 16, 1878).

    Russellville is the county town of Pope County, located on the Fort Smith and Little Rock R. R., containing about 1,000 inhabitants. We continued here some five or six weeks, and succeeded well, though I was sick a large portion of the time. We went from here to Dardenelle, a beautiful town on the southern bank of the Arkansas River. While here we were the guests of Judge Howel, and hospitably entertained by him and family. The preacher in charge, Brother Dodson, treated us with much kindness. He will ever have a place in our memory. We arrived here on Friday evening, and preached twice on the following Sunday to a large and attentive audience. On Monday, Tuesday and Wednesday nights I lectured to an appreciative audience, for which I received some $33 or $34 dollars. Taking leave of our kind friends we left for Atkins, a new town on the Fort Smith & Little Rock R. R. Passing through Russellville, we spent a day and a night with our friends and acquaintances. On reaching that place we were kindly received and became the guests of Esq. Ford. On the following night I delivered a lecture in the M. E. Church, South, and on the following Sunday preached twice. On Monday night I lectured in the Academy on "The English Language--the Importance of Its Study." A Grammar Class was formed for both day and night. We continued here some three or four weeks. Before leaving, I delivered a lecture on "Love," for which I was moderately remunerated. But upon the whole, we did well.

    Having wound up there, we left for Lewisburg, a town on the northern bank of the Arkansas River, about one mile south of the Fort Smith & Little Rock R. R. We left the railroad at a little village called Moulton. It contained only about twelve or fifteen families, but there were five drinking saloons with a gambling establishment in each. At Lewisburg we were domiciled with one Mr. Steel, formerly of this State, and kindly cared for by him and his family while we remained there. We were also receiveed by the preacher in charge and welcomed to his pulpit. On the following night preached in the Methodist Church. The weather being inclement, the congregation was not large. On the Saturday and Spnday following we attended a quarterly conference in the county, Brother Harrellson Presiding Elder, and both on Saturday and Sunday preached to an attentive audience. The Word had the desired effect, especially on Sunday. We returned Sunday evening to meet an appointment outstanding for that night. I delivered a lecture on "Love" on Tuesday night. Several ladies took a deep interest in the lecture, and voluntarily sold tickets, doing well; for whom the following verses were composed, and to whom they are dedicated:

AN APOSTROPHE TO WOMAN.

BY REV. B. YORK, D. D.

Oh, woman, it is thine to bless,
'Tis thine the aching heart to cheer;
'Tis thine to soothe in deep distress,
And wipe away the orphan's tear.

'Tis thine to shed the light of love,
On deepest grief that shrouds man's home,
As cheerful sunbeams from above
Scatter away night's sable gloom.

Of the sick room thou art the light,
To cheer the sick and make them well;
To chase away the gloom of night,
From the poor prisoner's loathsome cell.

Of man the boon of life thou art,

The central sun that makes home bright--
The balm of every wounded heart,
The star that gilds each scene with light.

When sorrow bows the spirit down,
Slow beats the heart by care oppressed;
Then by thy smile the light is sown,
That cheers and soothes the troubled breast.

Numbers thy value cannot tell,--
A gift from Heaven divinely fair;
For, in kind deeds thou dost excel,
As truth and mercy well declare.

(Atkins, Ark., April 1st, 1878.)

    We next visited Conway, a town on the same railroad, and here we met with rather a cold reception, for though the people knew we were coming, an appointment having been made for me to preach, no one met us at the depot, so we went to the hotel and there we stayed while we remained in town, for no one invited us out, though there was a full congregation at preaching. Here we met with the preacher in charge, but saw him no more until the day before we left, though we remained there some four or five days. I preached twice and lectured once, but made but little more than our hotel bill. From here we left for home, stopping over at Lone Oak, a town on the railroad, one night. I would have lectured but some kind of a show was in the way. The soil in this state is generally rich and abundantly productive, and the people generally liberal and kind. Academic schools are established in the most of the towns, but the system of public schools is very defective and inefficient. We reached home in North Carolina on the 20th of April, and found all well.

CHAPTER XXIII.

TEACHING AND LECTURING AT RUTHERFORD COLLEGE, HICKORY AND MORGANTON--AN EASTERN TOUR--SICK AT NEWTON--LECTURING AND PREACHING AT STATESVILLE--MOORESVILLE--SICK AT DAVIDSON COLLEGE--PREACHING IN CHARLOTTE--AT MONROE--BEAVERDAM--POLKTON--WADESBORO--HESITATING--LILESVILLE--ROCKINGHAM LAURINBURG AND LUMBERTON--IN SOUTH CAROLINA AT BENNETTSVILLE--FUNERAL SERMON--TEACHING CLASSES AT GILBOA, PINE GROVE, JERUSALEM--RETURN HOME.

I had now returned from my western tour without accomplishing the main object for which I went, viz.: to get funds to enable me to publish a new edition of the High School Grammar, which had been out of print some three or four years. Not willing to give up the object, I resolved to travel, lecture and preach with the view to accomplish this object.

I commenced lecturing at the college and met with some encouragement. I then lectured at Hickory and succeeded as well as I could expect. I then lectured and preached at Morganton, accomplishing something. In the meantime, through the exertions of my kind friend, Dr. G. B. Wetmore, I received letters of commendation from some of the leading men of the State, viz.: Governor Vance, Colonel Armfield, Major Robins, and others. Through the influence of these letters I obtained a free ticket on C. C. Railroad. On the 5th of June, '78, we set out on this preaching and lecturing tour, though so unusually unwell that I could scarcely sit up. The first appointment to preach and lecture was at Newton. We remained there three days, but I was so sick I could neither preach nor lecture. On Saturday the 8th, we left for Statesville, and on the next day, Sunday, preached twice, and lectured Monday night and received $10.00. On Wednesday the 12th we left for Mooresville, on that night at the request of the Rev. Mr. Penick, of the Presbyterian Church, on Religion, and on the following night lectured in the Academy on Love. It was well recived, and several dollars were collected. On Friday morning we left for Davidson College to fill an appointment there, but reaching there I was too sick even to sit up. On the next day we left for Charlotte, but no better. I went to bed as soon as one could be procured, but on Sunday morning I was much better, and preached twice in Tryon Street Church, Brother Bosshamer, preacher in charge. No opportunity offered for lecturing as schools were closing and every night was occupied. On Tuesday we left for Monroe. I was met at the depot by brother Thomas Kendall, a local preacher, and was conducted to his house where we were kindly treated and well provided for. My health, however, was still feeble, but I was able to preach on Wednesday night to a large congregation, and Friday night lectured in the Male Academy. The audience was not large, but intelligent and appreciative, there being some six or seven clergymen. A favorable notice of the lecture was published in the Monroe Enquirer. On Saturday brother Kendall took me some four or five miles into the country, and we spent the night with Colonel Rogers and his excellent wife. We were very kindly treated but I was too sick to enjoy anything. I was compelled to sit up the whole night without any means of relief. The next morning the good lady presented me with a two-dollar-and-a-half piece of gold. After breakfast we all set out for Shiloh Church to fill an appointment previously made for me to preach. A large congregation was assembled, though I was in a poor condition for preaching, but I preached as best I could. At the close, brother Kendall made a talk, took up a collection, and nearly twenty dollars were received. We returned to Monroe that evening, and had the pleasure of hearing Brother M. V. Sherrill preach. By request I lectured again on Tuesday night, and upon the whole in the way of money matters did well, but I saw not a well day while there. On Thursday morning we left for Beaver Dam, and I preached that night to a full congregation. An appointment having been sent on for me to preach at Gilboa Church in the country on Sunday, it also being the regular day for the preacher in charge, brother Rush, we went out next morning near the church to meet it. We were domiciled by the Widow Marsh, where we spent the night. The family was exceedingly kind, but I was too sick to enjoy anything. From two o'clock on Friday until sunset of Saturday I suffered intensely, and nothing could afford relief. About sunset the paroxysm ceased, and that night I rested well, and was greatly refreshed. Preached next day to a large attentive congregation. After the sermon brother Rush made a talk, took up a collection, and nearly thirty dollars were contributed. Next morning at nine o'clock I delivered a lecture on Education to a good house, and at night I lectured on Love, at Beaver Dam, and the house would not contain one half the people. A beautiful bouquet, together with fifty cents was presented me by an intelligent lady. Other contributions were made. On Tuesday morning, the 1st of July, we left for Polkton, an appointment having been made before. I preached on Tuesday night, and lectured on Wednesday night, and on Thursday the 4th of July we left for Wadesboro, where, according to appointment I was to preach on Thursday night and lecture on Friday night. We stopped at a hotel, as no other arrangement had been made, but we were cordially received and kindly treated, and were charged nothing. About two o'clock, P. M. I had a severe attack of asthma, which continued until 10 o'clock the next day. No remedy we had at hand would avail. Of course I did not preach. As soon as I was able to go we were taken to Mr. Edwards', a private family. His house was within a few rods of the Presbyterian Church. The church was offered to me for my use and I lectured at night to a good house, and was well remunerated. We were very kindly entertained by our host and hostess. Here we hesitated and consulted whether to return home or go on, for look which way we would nothing but gloom and darkness presented themselves. If we turned back we had nothing to go to, and to go on appeared almost impossible, for I was sick constantly. But we finally concluded to go on.

We left on Saturday, the 7th, for Lilesville, and reached there the same evening, and put up at the hotel, as no other arrangements had been made. The preacher in charge called on us, and told us the appointment was out for me the next day, but that he could not be present, as he had an appointment at another place. I preached twice on Sunday to a full congregation, and on Monday night lectured to a good house. Some attended from several miles in the country. We spent Monday and Monday night with brother Pepper in the parsonage, while my health began to improve, and I suffered no more with asthma for some two months. Our hotel bill was footed by two young men. We left Lilesville Tuesday morning for Rockingham; preached on Tuesday night and returned on Wednesday night. The congregation was good, and the collection amounted to $10. Several ministers were present, viz.: the preacher in charge, brother Guthrie, and Sanford, and Professor Neal. We left Rockingham for Laurinburg Thursday, and were met at the depot by brothers B. C. Philips, and Munday, the proprietor of the hotel, and were conducted to the hotel, where we were entertained. But as there was an exhibition that night I could not lecture. On Friday Brother Philips took us to a picnic in the neighborhood, where we found a large assembly collected. There were large provisions made for regaling the appetite and strengthening the physical man, but little for the mental or inner man. Next day he took me to two of his appointments. I preached at each appointment, sold some books, and received some donations. At night I lectured in Laurinburg to a large and appreciative congregation, and in a pecuniary way, did well. On Sunday I preached twice to large and attentive congregations. On Monday we went aboard for Lumberton. Brother May, preacher in charge, met us at the depot, conducted us to the parsonage, but arrangements had been made for accommodating us at the hotel, and in the evening we were conducted thither. I lectured on Monday and Tuesday night, and was to preach on Wednesday night, but the sexton neglected to ring the bell until nine o'clock, and I would not attempt to preach at that late hour. We found this to be a rather dull place. We did but little, though we were at no expense. On Thursday we took the other end of the road and stopped at Shoeheel, now Maxton. I preached on Thursday night, and lectured on Friday night, and succeeded much better than at Lumberton. Saturday we went aboard for Laurinburg, and fell in the quarterly meeting of brother Barrett, presiding elder. I preached on Sunday night to a large congregation. On Monday morning, July 22nd, we, Brother Phillips, the presiding elder, and several of the brethren and sisters, went to Caledonia church where a protracted meeting had been commenced a few days previous. On coming there we found quite a number of people had assembled. At the request of brother Philips, I preached, and the Lord was present to work, for quite a number of penitents approached the altar. The meeting continued several days, and I preached every day, and as well as I recollect, there were 30 or 40 converts, nor had the interest of the meeting still abated when it closed. On Wednesday night after the close, we went to Brother John's, the father of Rev. R. B. John, on the North Carolina Conference. On the following morning he sent us to Rev. William K. Bruden's, on the border of South Carolina.

    On arriving there, we found the family just ready to go to a meeting then in progress at Smyrna church. We found the junior preacher on circuit present, who requested me to preach, and I did so. There was quite a stir among the people, and several penitents were at the altar. I preached again in the afternoon, and continued preaching once and twice a day until after the Sabbath. On Sunday the congregation was very large and the weather disagreeably warm. Doubtless much good was accomplished during the meeting; the number of converts not recollected. On Sunday afternoon we went to Bennettsville, S. C., where an appointment was outstanding for me to preach. The rain prevented me from preaching. On Monday night I lectured to a full house, and was introduced to the audience by C. H. Huckabee, Esq., a young lawyer with bright prospects, who had graduated at Rutherford College while I was a professor in that institution. The next time I met him was in Smyrna Church in his coffin. I preached his funeral sermon from Sam. III.-27, "It is good for a man that he bear the yoke in his youth." He professed religion while at Rutherford College and joined the church. On Monday night I preached in the village, to a good congregation, and on Wednesday we returned to brother Burdon's. Thursday the 1st of August, I lectured to a large congregation at Pine Grove Church. A liberal contribution was made. We dined with the widow Betha near the church, with whom we spent the following 2 days. On Sunday morning the 4th of Aug. we went to St. John's Church to attend a protracted meeting, to redeem a promise made to brother Philips some weeks previous. On reaching there we found a very large congregation collected, and I preached to the people, and the seed sown appeared to fall in good ground, for there were several penitents, and 2 or 3 converts. Here I continued preaching once and twice a day, till Friday evening. The meeting was then dismissed as a campmeeting was to commence that night at Pine Grove only a few miles distant. The meeting was a success, and a liberal contribution was made. We returned to the widow Betha that evening. I preached on Saturday and Sunday of the campmeeting, was taken sick Sunday night, and preached no more until Wednesday afternoon. I then preached from the fall of Satan, and the effect was overwhelming, there being some fifty or sixty penitents at the altar, and as I left the stand a brother remarked to me, "the best wine has been kept for the last." As well as I recollect there were some 75 converts during the meeting. A grammar class had been here as the result of a lecture delivered on the Thursday preceding. I commenced on Friday morning, the session to be 20 days. It was taught under the arbor, a regular academical school was going on in the academy by Prof. Covington who exercised with the class as often as his duties would permit. During the continuance of the class, I continued preaching on Sunday at different places, and at the request of Prof. Covington and others, delivered 2 public lectures in the church. The class succeeded well and paid well. We then went to Beaverdam and were requested by Dr. Green to lecture and preach at Gilboa Church. The appointment was made for some 2 weeks hence, during that time I attended and preached at 2 protracted meetings, and one campmeeting, preaching every day at each. The time having arrived, I lectured at the appointed place, and a Grammar Class was readily formed, and I commenced teaching on the Monday following. The class was large with some eight or ten boarders. During the school session a protracted meeting was held at the church, and I preached several times. The day after the close of the class I visited Jerusalem, a church some 10 or 12 miles distant, preached on Saturday and twice on Sunday, and lectured on Monday. A grammar class was formed, and was to commence some 2 weeks hence. My health now had become bad and I was nearly run down, though I preached several times. We spent a week at Mathews Station with brothers Hammer and Abernethy, and then went and taught the class previously formed. While here I was requested by the colored people to preach to them. I did so and they manifested much pleasure, and as soon as the sermon was ended they came with their donations and laid them on the table and we found some three or four dollars. This school having closed we returned to Gilboa, and taught from the 1st of January until sometime in March, preaching on the Sabbath and sometimes by request at night. This school having closed we returned home and this terminated a nine months tour.

CHAPTER XXIV.

TEACHING LOGIC AND GRAMMAR AT THE COLLEGE--READING PROOF SHEETS AT MEBANESVILLE--RETURNING HOME TEACHING AT MILL GROVE--VISITING THREE CAMP MEETINGS--TEACHING AND LECTURING AT BETHEL--AT HOME, TEACHING LOGIC AND GRAMMAR--RETURNED TO BETHEL--TEACHING AT MILL GROVE, AT MATHEWS--RETURNED HOME.

Having accomplished my object, while corresponding with different publishing houses as to the publication of my Grammar, I taught classes in Grammar and Logic at the College. The Sabbaths were always employed in preaching at the College and other places.

A contract having been made with a publishing house in Raleigh, I, accompanied by my son Bascom, went to Mebanesville to read the proof sheets. On the same evening we arrived, was called on by Dr. Mebane and Major Bingham, who requested me to preach in the Presbyterian church that night. I did so and was employed to fill their pulpit during our stay as they were without a pastor at that time. I generally preached for them twice on Sunday; but occasionally preached at Lebanon, a Methodist church. While engaged in this work, I received a letter from a gentleman in Union Co. requesting me to teach a Grammar class at a church called Mill Grove, to commence a little after the middle of July. On our way home I preached and lectured at Company Shops, now Burlington. The time having arrived for commencing the class, I set out with my son Victor to meet the engagement. On Saturday before the beginning of the class, I delivered a public lecture and also preached on Sunday and commenced teaching on Monday, a large class having been formed. I continued teaching for 2 months, preaching on Sunday at different churches, attended a campmeeting at Zion, and also, at Bethel in Cabarrus Co, and also at Union Grove M. P. Church, preaching each day of the meeting while there. The school having closed at Mill Grove, we went to Bethel in Cabarrus Co., delivered a public lecture and formed a Grammar class for 20 days. As usual I preached on Sunday and lectured once a week on "Social Law and Etiquette." At the close of this class, another was formed to commence some time in Nov. We then returned home and continued there until time to commence the class. During the interval I taught classes in Logic and Grammar. The time having arrived we returned to Bethel to begin the class. [We] had a large class in English Grammar and a small one in Latin, lecturing once a week on "Social Law and Etiquette." We boarded in the Parsonage with Rev. M. H. Hoyle, of the North Carolina conference, where I taught a class at night in English and Latin. A little before the close of the class, Victor went home and Mrs. York came. I preached on Sabbath after the close of the class, while preaching I was taken quite sick and continued so for several days. As soon as I was able to travel, we went to Mill Grove, where a class had already been formed. We continued there 25 days, occasionally lecturing at night. While here I married 2 couples. After winding up here, we went to Mathews Station, preached and lectured, and formed a Grammar class for 25 days. In this place there were 3 churches, Baptist, Methodist, and Presbyterian, and a M. P. nearby. I generally preached twice on Sunday in all the churches except the Presbyterian. At the request of many, the night after the class had closed I delivered a lecture on Love in the Methodist church to a full audience. On Sunday before we left, I preached in the M. P. Church in the morning, and in the M. E. in the afternoon. The congregations were large, and deeply impressed. We then returned home.

CHAPTER XXV.

LECTURING AND PREACHING TOUR--LECTURING AND PREACHING AT NEWTON--AT CATAWBA STATION--AT STATESVILLE--AT LEXINGTON--AT YADKIN COLLEGE--AT THOMASVILLE--TRINITY COLLEGE--EBENEZER--RANDLEMAN--CEDAR FALLS--FRANKLINSVILLE--MEBANEVILLE--DURHAM--MOORESVILLE--RALEIGH--CLAYTON--SELMA--SMITHFIELD--CARY--CHAPEL HILL--COMPANY SHOPS--HOME.

On the first of May 1880, Mrs. York and myself left home on a preaching and lecturing tour. We met our first appointment at Newton, preached on Wednesday night and lectured on Thursday night. Had a full house to preach to, and would have been so at the lecture but for a thunder shower. But there were many more than was anticipated, and the lecture was quite a success. Brother Stamey the P. C. gave us his entire influence. From Newton we went to Catawba Station. There I lectured and preached, and for that place had a good house. On Saturday afternoon we left for Statesville. Preached on Sunday morning in the M. E. Church, South, and at night in the Presbyterian Church, and lectured on Monday night in the Methodist church. Bro. Hall, the pastor, and Bro. Wood of the Presbyterian Church took an interest in the lecture and gave me their entire influence. On Tuesday we left for Lexington. But reaching there in the night, we were conducted to a house through a mistake which had not been arranged by the brethren, for they had made preparation for our accommodation before our arrival. But General Leach and F. C. Robbins Esq. called on us early in the day, and arrangements were made for us to continue where we were.

Brothers Campbell of the Methodist church and Watson of the Presbyterian Church also called on us, and arrangements were made for me to preach in the Presbyterian Church. I preached to a large congregation, and the sermon was complimented by Gen. Leach and the Presbyterian preacher. Arrangement were made for me to lecture the next night in the Methodist Church, and in compliance with request I lectured to a very full house on "Education." At the close a liberal contribution was made. On the next day we went to Yadkin College and continued there several days. During our stay I preached twice, and lectured 3 times, and succeeded well. Bro. Simpson the Pres. of the College took a deep interest in both the preaching and lecturing. From here we went to Thomasville, and was [sic] happily domiciled with a kind friend Dr. Wetmore. I preached and lectured to a good house. From here we went to Trinity College, where in former years I had labored long and hard in establishing an academical school which, in after years, grew into a Normal College, and now Trinity College. On Sunday I preached to large intelligent audience, dined with Dr. Craven, and spent the evening pleasantly with his family. On Tuesday morning we were taken to Mr. Branson Coltrane's, a nephew of mine, and from there to Mt. Lebanon Church, where two Quaker preachers had an appointment to preach, a man and wife. We listened to both with much interest, but the woman was the better preacher. After they had closed, at the earnest solicitation of many, I also preached, so the people heard on that day what they seldom hear--3 preachers hold forth in succession. We had the pleasure of spending a few hours with this gentleman and his wife as we all dined together at Mr. Coletrane's, our relative. We were pleased with their plain, easy manners. We spent the balance of the week very pleasantly with Mr. Coltrane. On Sunday morning we took passage in the wagon, and all took a ride to Ebenezer Church, some 4 or 5 miles distant. I shall make no attempt to describe my emotions as I stood on that plot of ground, on which the house stands. It is not the same house, but the ground is the same. The reminiscences of years long gone by rushed into my mind like a flood. Here I saw the first campmeeting, and how strangely would these wooden tents built of round poles, compare with those tents of the present time. Here I was born again, and a few hours afterwards joined the Methodist Church, nearly 66 years ago, and continued a member at this place for some six or seven years, and was led by 3 class leaders consecutively, viz., Rev. Alson Gray, Franklin Harris, and Ahi Robbins. All these have crossed the flood. Soon after I joined the church the class became so large that it was divided into 3 sections, and a leader placed over each. Hence we had a class meeting every Sunday, one section meeting on each Sunday, and on the preaching day the pastor would meet the whole class. But where are the members, the Gassetts, the Grays, the Coletranes, the Smiths, the Robbinses, the Morgans, the Leaches and others, and the echo is where. The largest number has gone to the graveyard, for though I preached to a large congregation, perhaps not five of my contemporaries were present. I met with my old friend and brother Nathan Robbins, who was several years my senior. Our meeting was pleasant and he was much affected under my preaching. I also met with my friend and brother, Rev. Charley Philips of the N. C. Conference. In the graveyard lie my father and mother, my oldest sister and husband, James Coletrane. Also here I preached often in the early years of my ministry. Some 40 years had passed away since I was here before. From here we went to Randleman and fell in with a quarterly conference there on Saturday and Sunday, Dr. W. H. Bobbitt, P. E. On Sunday afternoon

I preached at Union Church, filling an appointment previously made. Here Mrs. York was taken sick, and we were detained some 2 weeks, and on Sunday morning I preached at St. Paul's and in the evening at Lebanon, the M. P. Church. Also during our stay I lectured in both churches. As soon as Mrs. York was able to travel, we went to Cedar Falls, and were very pleasantly entertained by bro Cox, of the M. P. church, and in his church I preached on one night, and lectured on the next to a full house each time, and $5 or $6 were contributed. From here we went to Franklinsville, and were domiciled with bro. Dennis Curtis, one friend among many, but since gone to his reward. An appointment was made for me to lecture on Saturday night, but I was taken quite sick, and was unable to fill it. On Sunday afternoon I attempted to preach, but my strength failing, I could not finish. During our stay here I preached twice, and delivered 2 public lectures, some $20 or $25 being contributed. We were then conveyed by brother Curtis to Greensboro, and all he charged was to make us a present of $5. Here we took the car for Mebaneville, and spent several days with our son William, during which time I preached and lectured at Lebanon church. We then took the train for Durham, and were met at the depot by brother F. H. Wood, the Pastor, and brother Walker, a local preacher. We were conveyed to the house of the latter, with whom we continued during our stay. On Sunday morning and night I preached in the Methodist church, and lectured on Monday night. The audience was not large as there was a political meeting in town at the same hour; but intelligent and appreciative, and I was liberally rewarded. On the day following we were met by our son Dr. N. D. York, and were taken to his house near O'Kelly's Chapel, and on the following Saturday and Sunday a two-day's meeting was held by Rev. W. G. Clements, and I preached on each day. From here we went to Morrisville, and preached on Friday night. From here we went to the city of Raleigh and were met at the train by Dr. L. Branson with whom we lodged during our stay. We were called on by Dr. Black in the evening and was requested to fill his pulpit on Sunday morning, a request was also sent for me to preach in Person Street church at night. Sunday came and I met both engagements.

We left Raleigh on Monday and stopped at Clayton, a village some 16 miles distant, and remained there some 2 days, but neither preached nor lectured. On the first night a large portion of the men were gone off on a fishing expedition and on the following night a thunder storm prevented. On Wednesday we went to Selma, and preached at night, on the next morning took the hack for Smithfield, some 4 miles distant, and stopped at the hotel where arrangements had been made for our accommodation. I preached at night to a good congregation, and lectured on the next night to as many people, and succeeded well. Here we met with Dr. Beckwith and several others with whom we had been acquainted some many years before, for I had preached there a week some 20 years previous. We left on Saturday morning, and went aboard for Cary, were met at the depot by Dr. S. Pool, were conducted to the hotel, where arrangements had been made for us. I preached twice Sunday and lectured on Monday night to a full house, and the contribution was liberal. I was strongly solicited to remain and lecture the following night, but could not accept because an appointment had been made for me to lecture that night at Morrisville. According to the appointment I lectured. Next morning we were met by our son, Dr. N. D. York, and taken to his house some 8 miles distant, and the next day he conveyed us to Chapel Hill. We continued there until the following Tuesday. On Sunday I preached twice to a very full congregation. While there we were called on by Pres. Battle, Dr. Mangum, Prof. Shepard of Baltimore who was then conducting the State Normal School, and several other gentlemen and ladies. On Tuesday we left, stopping a day or two at Mebaneville, then we went on to Company Shops (Burlington) to meet an appointment for preaching and lecturing. Rain prevented me from preaching; but lectured on the following night to a full house. On the next day (Saturday) we left for Greensboro. Were met at the depot and taken to the hotel kept by Mrs. Steel. Preached twice on Sunday to a very full congregation. On the following day we were called on by various gentlemen and ladies who made us various donations. On Monday evening we went aboard the cars for home, Rutherford College, where the N. C. Local Ministers' Conference met that year. Several preachers were in attendance and various subjects of interest were discussed. On Sunday I preached. This body of local ministers is doing much to improve their own helpfulness and consequently more for the church in aiding in "spreading scriptural holiness over these lands."

CHAPTER XXVI.

A WESTERN TOUR--PREACHING AND LECTURING AT NEBO--MARION--OLD FORT--ASHEVILLE--RESTING AT HON. R. B. VANCE'S--AT TURKEY CREEK CAMP AND DISTRICT MEETING--AT BURNESVILLE--HOME.

We remained at the College a few days only, and then set out for a western tour, appointments having preceded us at various places. We met the first one at Nebo church on the first Sunday in August. Preached to a good congregation, and lectured on the following day. It was well received and liberally rewarded. On Tuesday we went aboard for Marion, were met at the depot and conducted to the hotel where the brethren had arranged for us. On Tuesday night I preached to a full congregation, but was prevented from lecturing the following night by the fall of an abundance of rain. On Thursday we left for Old Fort, and were entertained at the hotel, kept by the widow Simonton, an acquaintance of ours, preached at night to a congregation as large as could be expected under the circumstances, as the streets were quite muddy. Lectured the following night to an attentive audience. On the next morning, being Saturday, we left for Asheville, and stopped at a hotel kept by widow Baird and Son. We were cared for during our stay and were charged nothing. Preached on Saturday to a large congregation at the request of brother Burnette, P. C. On the following Tuesday, the Hon. R. B. Vance, having heard that we were in town came and took us to his house where we spent 3 or 4 days very pleasantly.

Towards the last of the week we were sent to Turkey Creek Campground, where a District Conference and campmeeting were to be held in conjunction. We were gladly received and well cared for. This was an occasion of some interest there being some 30 or more ministers in attendance. Nearly every one that preached had his subject assigned some time previous by the P. E., Dr. Kenady. This increased the variety and interest of the occasion, but perhaps the effect would have been better if the preachers had selected their own subjects. I preached on Sunday to a large and attentive congregation. The sermon appeared to have a good effect. We were met there by Dr. Clontz, our son-in-law, and were conducted to Mr. John Clontz's, where he and my daughter lived, but before reaching there I was taken quite sick, and my health continued bad all the time I was west of the mountains, though on the Saturday following we went to Flat Creek Campmeeting, held by the M. P. Church. I preached on Saturday evening, but was not able to preach any more. On the following Sunday week, I preached at a Presbyterian church near Mr. Clontz's. We then went to Burnesville, a distance of some 35 miles. On Saturday afternoon after reaching there, at th rqust of Prof. J. E. Rheim, my son-in-law, I delivered a lecture on Education, and preached on the following day. On the following Sunday a protracted meeting commenced at which I preached each day while I remained. We left for home on the following Thursday. My health for some time continued feeble. I did comparatively little during the following winter.

CHAPTER XXVII. Spring of 1881.

NORTH CAROLINA CONFERENCE--PROHIBITION BILL PRESENTED TO PEOPLE BY LEGISLATURE--LECTURING ON PROHIBITION--AT TAYLORSVILLE, ROCKY SPRING--OLIN--EAGLE MILLS--JONESVILLE--ELKIN--YADKINSVILLE--SMITH GROVE--MOXVILLE--FARMINGTON--CLEMONSVILLE--YADKIN COLLEGE--LEXINGTON--THOMASVILLE--RANDLEMAN--FRANKLINSVILLE--COLUMBIA--CEDAR FALLS--NEW SALEM--HOME.

The North Carolina Conference during its session of 1880 passed a resolution memorializing the Legislature then in session, urging that body to adopt some measure or enact some law looking to the prohibition of the liquor traffic in the State. Similar documents in large numbers, poured in like a flood upon that body, so that, whatever may have been the sentiment of the members they were impelled to heed the voice of the petitioners; consequently a prohibition bill was framed to be submitted to the people for adoption or rejection. This having been done, prohibition clubs were organized throughout the State, and preparations were made for a vigorous campaign against the common foe, King Alcohol, who was strongly fortified, being surrounded by a wall built of dollars and cents almost impeneterable to argument, or to the tears of women and the moans of orphans. A prohibition club of many members was organized at Rutherford College, and regularly officered, holding its meetings weekly. At these meetings various plans were proposed and discussed, looking to the best plan to accomplish the object in view. This club requested me at the proper time to take the field and advocate the cause of prohibition. To this I readily consented, having for more than half a century advocated the cause of Temperance, looking to the desirable end, Prohibition. I was requested to ask people whom I addressed for voluntary contributions to aid in accomplishing the object in view. On the night before setting out on the campaign, I addressed a large audience in the college chapel on the subject of Prohibition, and some 7 or 8 dollars were contributed for the object. Accordingly on the next day, the 30th of April, I set out with Dr. Clontz, my son-in-law, as my traveling companion, to meet various appointments which had been sent on. We met the first at Taylorsville at night. There was a tolerably good house. After the lecture voluntary contributions were made. On the next morning, Sunday, we went to Rocky Spring Church to meet an appointment for preaching. I preached twice on that day, and addressed a full audience Monday night, and not a little enthusiasm was manifested. On the next day we went to Mount Pisgah in Iredell County, but the appointment having failed to reach that place nothing was done. On the next day we went to Olin High School, where we found a considerable collection of people. I addressed them on prohibition, much interest was manifested, and a liberal contribution was made. On the next day, Thursday the 5th, we went to Eagle Mills, and at night addressed a very large audience, the contribution made was unusually liberal. On the following night I preached to a large congregation. On the following day we went to Jonesville, Yadkin County, and preached to a full congregation at night. On the next day, Sunday the 8th, we went to Elkin and I preached twice to a large congregation, and on Monday night addressed a large audience on Prohibition, and a liberal contribution was made.

We returned the next day to Jonesville, and at the request of Brother Cheely, delivered a lecture in the morning on Education, and at night addressed a very full audience on Prohibition. On the next day, Wednesday the 11th we went to Yadkinville, and at two o'clock P. M. addressed a large audience on Prohibition in the Court House, and preached, also, in the same house at night. On Thursday we went to a small village called Andersonville in Davie County, and addressed at night a tolerably fair audience, but not one cent would they give for the cause, and I would remark once for all that this was the only place that refused to give anything to aid in carrying out the campaign. On Friday we went to Smith Grove where I addressed a large audience on Prohibition, and on Saturday we went to Mocksville at which place the county held a Prohibition Convention where there was a goodly number assembled. I addressed the convention in the afternoon, and it is worthy of remark as the thing was very rare, that only 2 ladies were present. We returned to Smith Grove the same evening, and on the next day, Sunday the 15th, preached to a crowded house. At the close of the sermon, several liquor dealers among others, came to me and made liberal contributions, remarking that they were willing to pay for the preaching, if not for the lecture. At 3 o'clock P. M., I preached to a congregation at a church called Olive Branch, and that night we were domiciled with an old friend and brother, Wesley Johnson whose acquaintance I had made some 40 years before. The next day we spent with Mr. James Johnson who had been a student of mine at Clemonsville; and at night in the temperance hall at Farmington, I addressed a packed house, and much interest was manifested for Prohibition. At this place there was a temperance organization, and had been for years. On Thursday we went to Clemonsvville where I had officiated as principal of a high school for several years, and at night preached to a large audience. On the next day we dined with the widow of

Dr. McKeever, she and 2 others were all I found who were adults when I lived there. At night I addressed a large audience on Prohibition, and some enthusiasm was manifested. On the following day we went to Yadkin College, and on Sunday the 22nd preached to a very large audience in the college chapel, on Monday night addressed a full crowd on Prohibition, and much interest was manifested. This being the Commencement week we continued several days. On Friday at the request of several, I lectured on Education, and on Sunday went out with bro. Lowe and preached for him at one of his churches. On Monday night the 30th, I lectured on Prohibition to a good house at Lexington, and on Tuesday the 31st we went to Thomasville, and there fell in with the Commencement of the Female Seminary. At night we heard Dr. Wilson preach the Annual Sermon, and the following day deliver the literary address. On Thursday we left, calling a while at Trinity College, but as the President, Dr. Craven said they were all Prohibitionists, I did not lecture but left for Branson Coltrane's and there spent the night and following day. On Saturday the 4th of June we went to Marlberry a Quaker church, at which time and place the Friends were holding quarterly meeting. By invitation I addressed the people on the subject of Prohibition which was listened to with marked attention, and let it here be said in honor of the Friends, they are a unit on Prohibition. The same evening we went to Randleman, and were domiciled with our friend Dr. W. A. Woolen, and the next day we preached in Saint Paul's Church, B. C. Philips pastor, and at night in Lebanon the M. P. Church. We spent the night with James Caudle Esq., and during the night I was taken very unwell. On the next day, though hardly able to sit up, I went to Asheboro to attend the County Prohibition Convention, though too unwell to attend all the exercises of the occasion. In the evening we went to Randleman. After a few hours' rest though still sick, I addressed a very large audience in the town hall. On the next day we went to New Salem, stopping with Esq. Caudle where we remained several days as I was too sick to travel. On Saturday the 11th we went to Franklinsville, and at night addressed a good house on Prohibition, and preached on the next day. On Monday we went to Columbia Factory, addressed the people at night on Prohibition, and some interest was manifested. According to arrangement we returned to Franklinsville, and stopped with Esq. Horney an old and tried friend. Ample preparations were made for our accommodation, but I was to sick to enjoy anything. In the afternoon we went to Cedar Falls to meet an appointment previously made, and at night, though quite sick, I addressed a very large audience in the M. P. Church. On the next day (Wednesday) we returned to New Salem. As my health had become too bad for travelling, I taught a Grammar class at that place for 20 days, during which time I preached on Prohibition at Level Cross and at Lebanon in Randleman. I also preached in St. Paul's but not on that subject.

During the teaching of this class I was solicited by the citizens generally to establish a high school at this place, to which I consented, and at night after the class had closed I lectured to the citizens in the hall on that subject, when it was resolved to commence the school in the Masonic Hall on the 10th of August. A committee was appointed to prepare it for the school. This having been arranged, we set out for home and were domiciled with Mr. John Aldridge that night. I was quite sick when I reached there, but Mrs. Aldridge was very kind and did all she could for me. Next morning, Sunday, we set out for Thomasville, but failed to get there in time to attend the morning service at the church, but at night at the request of the pastor, J. J. Renn, I preached in the Methodist Church, and at the request of many lectured on Prohibition on Monday night. Some 5 or 6 ministers were present, and much interest was manifested. Next day the 12th of July we set out for home, and spent the night at Mocksville with brother Coon, the Pastor whose health was rapidly declining, and who in a few months died. On the 14th I reached home, preached some two or three times on Prohibition, and also on other subjects. The election came on. The Rutherford College township went largely for Prohibition, but in the State it was lost by a large majority. But, however, much was done for the great cause of the home and nation.

CHAPTER XXVIII.

OPENING OF NEW SALEM AND RANDLEMAN HIGH SCHOOL--EDUCATIONAL ASSOCIATION--MOVING INTO THE NEW BUILDING--THE SCHOOL IN A FLOURISHING CONDITION--RESIGNATION OF THE PRINCIPAL, PROF. RHEIM AND PROF. YORK.

On the 10th day of August, 1881, the first session of the school subsequently known as New Salem and Randleman High School was opened, some 24 or 25 scholars being enrolled. My son Bascom was associated with me as teacher. We commenced teaching in the old Masonic Hall, and continued there for about one half of the session. The school was then removed to the Quaker church. The first session closed on the day before Christmas. A public examination was held on the afternoon of the last day. The school was addressed by Maj. R. W. York, A. M., of Chatham Co., and an exhibition was held at night. The exercises consisted of Dialogues, declamations, and colloquies. The students performed well for the time, and a very favorable effect was produced for the school. The second session began on the first Wednesday in January, '82. The number of scholars was considerably increased. Lectures were delivered by the Principal through the session on Moral and Social Law. A literary society was, also, organized, known as the Ransomian Literary Society. As Davidson Victor York took a very active part in its organization, and in collecting books for the library, a gold medal was awarded him by the society for the highest number of books donated. At the close of this session, a public examination was held. The annual sermon was preached by Rev. G. B. Wetmore, D. D., of Rowan County, and the literary society was addressed by G. S. Bradshaw, Esq., of Asheboro. The attendance was large, and at night the exercises consisted of Declamations, Dialogues and Colloquies. Mr. Alfonso Ellison of Greensboro was awarded a book, having received the highest grade as a declaimer, also Miss Zorada Ingold, of Yorkville, S. C., a book as the best performer. Just after the close of the first session a meeting in the interest of the school was held in Randleman, and an Educational Association was organized. Rev. B. C. Philips was elected President, T. C. Worth, Esq., Secy, and Mr. J. H. Furee, Treas. I was elected Principal of the School and agent and my son Bascom was elected Professor of Latin and Mathematics in the Institution. It was resolved by the Association to erect a suitable building, and a building committee was elected to carry into effect the resolution. Trustees were, also, elected. During the vacation, Bascom and I attended the Local Ministers' Conference at Raleigh. I preached by appointment at 11 o'clock on Sunday, and also preached at several places, and solicited donations for the school building. The third session opened the first of Aug, and as the new building was not completed, the church was still occupied by the school. The number of scholars was considerably increased at the opening of this session. Before the close of the session, the new building was completed, and the school removed into it. The building was large and well adapted to school purposes. It was 60 by 40 feet, with chapel below, and 5 rooms for recitation above. One room was assigned to the Literary Society. During this session, Mr. M. M. Lemond, of Union Co., entered the school, and was employed, also, as teacher of Penmanship and Vocal Music. The session closed with a public examination and, also, exercises at night.

The 4th session as usual opened the 1st of Jan, '83. At the opening of this session the outlook was truly flattering, some 24 or 25 boarders in attendance, and during the session between 70 and 80 scholars were enrolled. The Literary Society was in a very flourishing condition. Their hall was furnished with suitable seats, the floor carpeted, and the room painted, and a chandelier to illuminate it, also, a library of nearly 200 volumes. The faculty (was) full and success attended every department of teaching. A gold medal was put up for the best declaimer among the boys, and, also, one to be awarded to the best reader among the girls. The commencement came off the last of May. The first day of the occasion was spent in the examination of the students who acquitted themselves well. At nine o'clock on the second day, Prof. Lemond's class in Vocal Music were examined and exercised on several pieces of music. At 11 o'clock Dr. W. M. Roxley of the N. C. Conference, preached the Annual Sermon. To say that this sermon was good hardly expresses its intrinsic value. It was very highly spoken of by those who heard it. At 3 o'clock P. M. Professor Pegram of Trinity College, delivered the Literary Address. It was a sensible and impressive discourse. During the interval between the Sermon and the Address the Educational Association met, when Capt. J. E. Rheim, A. M., of Burnesville, N. C., was elected Professor of Mathematics. It was, also, resolved that the Principal of the school should address the audience on the financial needs of the Association and take up a collection. This was done according to order, and between $100 and $200 were received. Other gentleman called on made complimentary remarks. At night the Exhibition and contests for the medals came off. The exercises as far as we could learn, gave universal satisfaction. J. M. Coltrane, having received the highest grade in declamation, the gold medal was presented to him by Rev. B. C. Philips and Miss Zula C. Hays having received the highest grade in reading, was presented with a gold medal by the same person. The audience was large, there being a good attendance at every hour's service. The audience was dismissed with the benediction by Rev. B. C. Phillips. The 5th session opened early in August. At the opening of this session there was a large increase of scholars, nearly 100 were enrolled during the term. As Prof. Rheim failed to get in at the beginning, D. V. York was employed to aid in teaching. A teacher in Instrumental Music was, also, employed, but soon proved himself unworthy of the situation, and consequently was relieved of his position. The Institution now appeared to rest on a firm basis, and in a fair way to soon be out of debt. The session had far advanced before Professor Rheim took his position. The session closed with the usual Elocutionary Exercises. A gold medal was up for the best declaimer. The declamation was unusually good. Mr. W. C. Armfield of S. C., having received the highest grade, the medal was presented to him by Mr. D. V. York.

Up to this time the school gradually increased in numbers every session; but a reverse now waited it. The 6th session opened the first of Jan. '84, but a financial crisis having fallen upon the Manufacturing Companies, and the prevalence of the measles in the school and all around in the country, reduced the number of scholars to less than half the preceding session. But as these causes would ultimately cease, little doubt was entertained of the future prosperity of the Institution.

At the opening of this session Miss Bettie Bulla of Greensboro took her position as teacher of Instrumental Music, and was succeeding well, giving lessons on the Piano in the day, and on the Guitar at night. She was a young lady of fine attainments, and could pass well in any literary circle. She, however, was attacked by the measles, and was confined to her room for nearly three weeks. On recovering she left for home. The number of scholars being so much smaller than usual, Prof. B. A. York left and taught a school in Wake Co. Though the neighborhood patronage had fallen off so much, the number of boarders held up well, having lost but few. Notwithstanding the number of scholars had been greatly reduced, yet the interest of the school had lost but little. The Commencement came off the last of May. On the first day of the occasion a public examination of the students was held. The students never acquitted themselves better. Rev. Pickette of the M. P. church preached the Annual sermon, and the Literary Address was delivered by Maj. R. W. York, A. M., of Chatham County. Both the sermon and the address were appropriate and were well received by the audience. At night elocutionary exercises came off, and a contest for a gold medal among the boys. Mr. O. Y. Rheim was the successful one, and won the medal. The exercises were scarcely ever more interesting or the declamation better. During the commencement occasion the Educational Association held its annual meeting, Rev. Amos Gregson in the chair. The Principal refused to serve longer without reelection, and it being put to a vote of the Association, he was unanimously re-elected Principal. Prof. Rheim and Prof. B. A. York resigned, Prof. Lemond having resigned during the session. Now came the tug of war, and the fate of the Institution trembled in the balance. Some discontented spirits had been during the last session sowing the seeds of discord, and some who had been the most active and self-sacrificing in the building up of the Institution, were now, though perhaps not intentionally, equally active in pulling it down. A union having been formed among the former friends, [and] the avowed enemies of the school, caucuses were held here and there as if everything depended upon their plans and actions. They finally succeeded in causing the Principal to resign his position as Principal and agent. Another dollar, perhaps, was never collected for the Institution. They finally succeeded in employing Professor Brooks and wife, of Olin, but Professor Brooks proved to be unpopular as a teacher, and a single session wound up the ball, and that session was the last.

CHAPTER XXIX.

A TOUR INTO SOUTH CAROLINA--TEACHING CLASSES, PREACHING AND LECTURING--PUBLISHING COMMON SCHOOL GRAMMAR--THROWN FROM A BUGGY, SERIOUSLY HURT--VISITING HIS CHILDREN IN WAKE, CHATHAM AND ORANGE COUNTIES--AT HOME AGAIN.

On the 2nd day of June, '84, Bascom and I left New Salem en route for Tradesville, S. C., and reached there on Saturday, the 7th, and were pleasantly domiciled with Dr. Dorster, a gentleman with whom Mrs. York and I had boarded some three months in Union Co, N. C. Several gentlemen called on us and engagements were made for preaching the next day. In the morning, at the request of the Baptist minister, Rev. Mr. King, I preached in the country some four or five miles from the village, and at 3 P. M. I preached to a large congregation in the Baptist church at the village. The audience seemed to be impressed with the sermon and I trust some good was done. On the following Monday night, I lectured in the same church with a view to forming a Grammar Class. The Class being formed, we commenced teaching on Thursday the 12th. On the following Sunday I preached again in the Baptist church. On the following Sunday (22) I preached at Tabernacle, a Methodist church, out in the country. On the 29th I preached in a church in the morning, and my son Bascom preached in the evening, place not recollected, and on Sunday, July 6, I preached again at Tabernacle. During the session I delivered two public lectures, for which some remuneration was received. On the 10th we had a public examination of the class, having taught twenty-five days. The students acquitted themselves nobly. On the following day we left for Mill Grove Church in Union Co, N. C. where a class had already been formed. I delivered a lecture on Saturday the 12th, and preached on Sunday morning, and in the afternoon at a church some six or seven miles distant. On Monday the 14th we began teaching, having enrolled thirty scholars. On the following Saturday and Sunday the Quarterly Conference was held at this church, Rev. T. M. Guthrie, P. E. I preached on Sunday to a large, attentive congregation and not without effect. On Sunday, the 27th, I preached at the same church. On the following Saturday I attended a Sunday school picknick at little Bethel. My son Victor having come to me, my son Bascom left for home. In the forenoon I delivered an address to the audience, and brother Caraway of the N. C. Conference delivered one in the afternoon. On the following day I preached to a large congregation in the morning and Victor in the evening. On Wednesday, the 6th, the first session of the school closed with a public examination, and another class was formed. During this session I visited two camp-meetings. On Saturday the 30th of August the term closed, at which time we had a public examination both on Grammar and Logic. The students acquitted themselves well, and the impression made on the audience was favorable. On Sunday the 31st I preached at Wesley's Chapel, Union Co., N. C., and on the following day delivered a public lecture on "The English Language, The Importance of its Study." There was a good audience, and a class was readily formed. On the 2nd day of Sept we commenced teaching, nearly 30 scholars in attendance. I preached several times at different places during the session. This class closed in twenty days, and another was formed. The commencement was put off some three or four days in order to revise and correct the Common School Grammar, as another edition was called for. Victor now went to Raleigh to attend to the printing of the book, and I commenced teaching the class on Monday, Sept. 29, and on Saturday, the 4th of Oct., returning from the class in a buggy with Miss Reid, a young lady, the horse ran away, and I was thrown out and very seriously hurt. Miss Reid fell out but was not seriously hurt. I was so badly hurt that for some hours I was entirely unconscious of what had occurred, my right arm being broken and my wrist out of place. I was confined for several weeks. Victor having returned from Raleigh finished teaching the class. As soon as I was able to go out I delivered a public lecture at Stony Wall. A class was formed for Victor. I preached for the first time after being hurt at a Quarterly Conference at Wesley's Chapel. I then went to Monroe where I continued teaching forty days, and only preached once during the time. While here Mrs. York was taken sick and was closely attended by Dr. Isaac Blair, but he would receive no compensation. Having wound up here I went to White Plains, S. C., I lectured on Saturday and preached on Sunday in the Baptist church, and in compliance with a request delivered a public lecture on Monday. A class of some 17 or 18 was formed. Before this session had closed, Victor had left for home. After it had closed Mrs. York and I went to Jefferson, lectured and formed a class. During the time of this class I preached at several places. The class having closed, we set out on the last day of February 1885 for home. Preached at Gilboa church on the 1st of March. On the following Wednesday we went aboard the train for New Hill Wake Co., and were met there by our son, Maj. York, and conducted to his house. We preached on the following day, Sunday, at Mount Pisgah, a Baptist church. In the evening I preached to a congregation of colored people, and by request preached to the same on the following Wednesday night, and the following Sunday preached at O'Kelley's Chapel. We continued here with our sons, Maj. R. W. York, and Dr. N. D. York some three or four weeks, preaching at different places on the Sabbath, and sometimes in the week, and, also, once to the Colored people. Our visit through here, we took the train for Bingham School, and were met by William York, our son, and taken to his house. But on the way I was taken very sick, and continued sick for several days, so that I only preached once during our stay. We then left for Greensboro, and were met by Victor and taken to our home at New Salem about the middle of April, my health being still bad.

CHAPTER XXX.

TRAVELING FOR MY HEALTH--AT GREENSBORO--REIDS VILLE--LEAKSVILLE--AT HOME AGAIN.

After reaching home an appontment was made for me to preach on the following Sunday, notwithstanding my health was still delicate. But on sunday morning while walking alone I by some means stumbled and fell with my face on a rock, and was so badly hurt that I could not preach, but I improved so much that I preached at night. We continued at New Salem until about the first of May. My health continued to decline. It was thought that by travelling, changing location and air I might improve my health. Mrs. York and I therefore left New Salem and went to Greensboro, and stopped with brother Ingal, but my health improved none. I not only suffered with Asthma, but my general health seemed almost gone. On the Friday following we went aboard the train for Reidsville, and were met at the depot by one of the brethren, and were conducted to a boarding house where arrangements had been made for our accommodation, but I was still sick. Dr. Bruton, Pastor of the Methodist Church, called on us that evening, but I was too unwell to make any arrangements for either lecturing or preaching. On Sunday morning some of the brethren requested me to make a talk to the Sunday School. I delivered a short lecture to the school, and consented for an appointment to be made for me to preach at night. At the hour I went to the church and found a large congregation assembled. I preached a short sermon, and was scarcely able to walk back to our boarding house, only about 100 yds distant. I now had to give up, and on Monday morning Dr. Courts was called in. He gave me close attention for several days, visiting me twice and sometimes three times a day. Towards the last of the week my health had somewhat improved, and on Saturday morning we left for Leaksville and were domiciled with brother Daniel Field a local preacher, a relative of my first wife. On Sunday morning I preached to a full congregation in the Presbyterian church, and by request of brother Field and others an appointment was made for me to lecture in the Methodist church on Prohibition on Tuesday night, but the inclemency of the weather and the state of my health prevented my filling the engagement. A young man present of only 19 or 20 heard me preach and it was his last, as he was buried on the following Sabbath. On Friday we returned to Reidsville and were entertained at the hotel, Dr. Bruton having made the arrangement before we arrived. On Saturday morning we took the cars for Greensboro. We were met at the depot by brother Ingold, and were conducted to his house. We went to church Sunday morning and heard brother Crawford, the Pastor of the M. E. Church, South. Announcement was made for me to preach at night, and at the hour appointed I preached to a very large congregation. Brother Crawford thanked me for the sermon, and said he believed good was done. Of the sermon and the man the following notice was published in the Greensboro Patriot, and copied by a great many other papers of the state:

* Clipping was not found in the Mss. [Editor]

On the Tuesday following we returned to New Salem, my health being a little improved.

CHAPTER XXXI.

A TOUR TO THE MIDDLE OF THE STATE--TEACHING A GRAMMAR CLASS AT MORRISVILLE--LECTURING AND TEACHING AT VARIOUS PLACES-- ENGAGED IN PROTRACTED MEETINGS AT VARIOUS PLACES--RETURN HOME.

Soon after we returned home, I received a letter informing me that a Grammar class had been or would be made at Morrisville and that it was thought advisable for me to come down some time before the commencing of the class, and preach and lecture at different places throughout the neighborhood. Consequently about the middle of June Mrs. York and I left for that place. We stopped at Mebanesville, and spent a few days with our son William, during which time I preached on the Sabbath at Lebanon Church. We then went aboard the train for Morrisville, and were met at the depot by our son Dr. York, and escorted to his house. On the same evening Maj. York came down and next morning we went with him to his house, and on the following Saturday night, (26th of June) I delivered a public lecture at Berea, a Baptist church, some eight miles distant, and on the next day preached to a very large audience in the same church, Rev. Matthew Farrell, the pastor, being present. On this occasion as well as all others where I met him, his bearing towards me was that of a Christian gentleman. Also, an appointment was outstanding for me to preach at Mount Pisgah at 5 o'clock, a distance of some eight or ten miles; so I had but little time for refreshment or resting. I met the appointment and preached to a large congregation. After the sermon a lady remarked to me, "You look very feeble." I answered, "Yes, and I suppose I feel as feeble as I look," for my health was still far from being good. On the following Sabbath, the 1st Sunday in July, I preached at Morrisville in the Christian church, and in the evening at a church in the country, the name of which I have forgotten. On reaching the place we found a large audience, so that the house would not contain more than half of them. However, the people were attentive and orderly. After the sermon we went to Maj. York's, much fatigued. On the second Sunday of July, I preached at Massey's Chapel, and, also, on the day before, being the appointment of the P. C. Who failed to come. On sunday evening at four o'clock, I preached to a large colored congregation in the vicinity of Mount Pisgah Church. On the following Tuesday night I delivered a public lecture in Morrisville. A class having been formed I be-began teaching the next day. On the following Sunday I preached in a Baptist church some four miles in the country, and in the evening at 3 P. M., preached to a large colored congregation at Bethel church near the railroad. The people appeared to be very much impressed with the sermon, and at the request of the pastor they took up a collection to remunerate the preacher. On the following Sunday, brother W. G. Clements commenced the series of meetings in Morrisville. He was assisted by Rev. Jeremiah Holt, of Burlington. During the meeting I preached three times. It continued until Friday night following without much visible good. On the following Sunday I went to Mount Pisgah, and at the request of the pastor preached at 11 o'clock. The sermon was highly complimented by brother Willson, the Pastor. As I could not remain longer in consequence of the school, I returned to Morrisville the same evening. On the following Saturday the Baptists commenced their meeting in Morrisville. I preached for them on Sunday and no more. It continued some 10 or 11 days though there were but few converts. I taught two sessions or forty days at this place. A gold medal was put up by Miss Lillie York for the one who stood the best examination. The donor required that the class should be examined two days, and Miss Minnie Herndon having received the highest grade, the medal was awarded to her and presented by Maj. York in a very impressive and appropriate speech. Just before the class closed, I received a letter from my son William, requesting me to attend a protracted meeting at Lebanon church. We left Morrisville on Wednesday morning before day and reached the church the same day as the meeting was in progress. It continued through the following Sunday, during which time I preached six times. The meeting was a success. On Sunday the crowd was very large, and I preached twice, Rev. L. L. Johnson, the pastor, having left. After the close of the services, I was presented with a donation of some $7 or $8. In a few days, we left and returned to our home at New Salem.

CHAPTER XXXII.

ATTEND THE PROHIBITION CONVENTION IN GREENSBORO--RESTING AT MEBANESVILLE--TEACHING SCHOOL AT NEW SALEM--PREACHING ON THE SABBATHS--TAKE CHARGE OF A SCHOOL AT FAIR VIEW--LECTURING AND PREACHING--VISITS DOBSON CIRCUIT AND ROCKY SPRINGS CAMP MEETING--LABORING IN PROTRACTED MEETINGS.

On reaching home, as stated in the preceding chapter, I found Victor teaching a small school, but as he was desirous of prosecuting his Theological Studies, I took charge of the school, aided by his wife, and preached generally on Sunday at New Salem or Randleman. On the 3rd of October a campmeeting of the M. P. Church began at Level Cross. I preached on Sunday to a large and appreciative congregation, and returned home that evening but Victor returned to the meeting on Tuesday, and in the afternoon of that day the work greatly revived, and I was sent for to aid in conducting the meeting. The preacher in charge and all the rest except a young preacher had left. Victor and I continued it through the following Sunday, during which time I preached once or twice every day. There was a gracious work; as well as I recollect, there were some forty converts. I continued teaching this small school until nearly Christmas, and as nothing special was on hand we devoted the time in writing on my Autobiography. On the 20th of Jan., two gentlemen came from East Guilford and solicited us to take charge of a new academy called Fair View, and on the 26th we set out for the purpose of doing so, and on Jan. 28th '86, we began teaching. A young man had previously been engaged to teach the public school, but as he proved to be inadequate to the task, he was relieved, and we finished the Public School, which lasted nearly two months. Then a regular Academical School was organized, and, as I did not wish to be troubled with the government of the school, Victor acted as principal. There were no Methodists in the community. There were three prominent denominations, viz. German Reformed, Presbyterians, and Lutherans. As the last mentioned had a school of their own, they had but little to do with our school. We were however, very kindly treated by our neighbors, and conveyance was readily furnished for us wherever we wished to go. I delivered lectures on Social Law and Etiquette on Saturday evenings nearly through the whole session, and we were pleasantly accommodated; for a house was soon erected on the Academy grounds for us. The lectures were well attended and remunerated. In short, the school was prosperous and promising. We had regular preaching in the Academy and occasionally I preached both for the Presbyterians and

German Reforms. Towards the close of the session I preached two sermons on Scriptural Prohibition. This question was now agitated more or less throughout the county of Guilford. The liquor traffic was the only thing that threatened the school. Almost in sight of the Academy ardent spirits were sold by retail, in violation of the law. The people of the neighborhood were divided on the subject of Prohibition. The German Reform Church was a unit on the subject of Temperance, but the Presbyterian congregation, unlike any other Presbyterian congregation I ever knew, was almost a unit in opposition to Prohibition, notwithstanding their pastor, the Rev. Mr. Miller, was sound to the core on temperance, and preached in favor of total abstinence and Prohibition. But there was a cause of the opposition of this people; for nearly all of this congregation once belonged to the German Reformed; but as this church passed a law prohibiting its members from having anything to do in the traffic of spirituous liquors, either drinking, selling or manufacturing it, the liquor element then left and built a church called Spring Wood, within one mile of the Academy, and joined the Presbyterian church. It is true, however, that there were very many clever members belonging to this Presbyterian congregation. The first session of the school was now hastening to a close, and the Commencement embraced the 3rd and 4th of June. Notwithstanding it was a busy season, yet the patrons prepared well for the occasion. The first day was occupied in examining the classes, and was well attended by the patrons and neighborhood generally, and they appeared to be much gratified at the proficiency made by the students. On the second day a very large audience was in attendance. Dr. Klapp, of Newton, preached the Annual Sermon in the morning. His subject was "The Out-look of the World." His text, "Watchman, what of the night?" It was a masterly production, and made a favorable impression. At one o'clock, P. M., Maj. R. W. York delivered the Literary Address. It was rich in thought and eloquent in language. Then came off the contest of the young men for a gold medal. A very intelligent committee was selected to grade the speakers, and award the medal. The declamation was unusually good. As all had declaimed well, the committee had some difficulty in deciding on the respective merits, but the medal was finally awarded to Mr. Charley C. Linebery, of Guilford. The music was good. The whole of the exercises were interesting and instructive. At the close Dr. Klapp made some complimentary remarks concerning the exercises. It was then announced that the second session would open on the first Wednesday in August, the audience was then dismissed with the benediction by Dr. Klapp. During the vacation Mrs. York and I visited Bascom on his work on the Dobson circuit, and continued there until the last of July, during which time I preached twenty times at different churches on his work. We went from here to Rocky Springs Campmeeting in Alexander county. My health had become bad, but I preached one sermon during the meeting. After spending a week or two with our son Clegg and daughter Rachel Eliotte, we returned to Fair View, the session having opened some ten days before we arrived. This session was much smaller than was anticipated. When we reached home we found a protracted meeting going on at the Presbyterian church. I attended, and at the request of the Pastor, preached three days in succession. The meeting was a success. I, also, attended a protracted meeting at the Brick church of the German Reforms. Was kindly received by the pastor, Dr. Welker, and took an active part in the preaching during my stay. The meeting was a success, resulting in some forty or fifty converts. I also visited a protracted meeting at Mount Pleasant church, Rev. J. A. Bowles pastor. I preached on Sunday morning, and Victor in the evening. The meeting as I learned resulted in quite a number of converts. In the meantime I attended the prohibition convention in Greensboro, and by request made a speech before the convention. There was a larg attendance, and several speeches delivered. I also attended a Quarterly Conference at Holts Chapel, Rev. J. A. Cuninggim P. E. The meeting was protracted and continued through the following Sabbath. I preached frequently during the meeting. Brother Jones, a Quaker preacher, also aided. Though good was done and some were converted yet there was a serious drawback on account of an existing difficulty between some of the principal members. Victor having determined to join Conference resigned his position when the session was only half out, and soon after Mrs. York and I went to our son William's at Mebanesville, N. C.

CHAPTER XXXIII.

CELEBRATES HIS GOLDEN WEDDING--VISITS DOBSON CIRCUIT--TEACHING, LECTURING AND PREACHING--VISITING BREVARD CIRCUIT--PREACHING, FREQUENTLY--VISITING DAUGHTERS IN YANCEY AND BUNCOMBE COUNTIES--AT HOME IN ALEXANDER COUNTY--VISITS BASCOM'S WORK IN STANLEY COUNTY.

In a few days after our arrival at William's, the day of our Golden Wedding arrived, viz., Nov. 13, 1886, but the children were so scattered and pursuing so many different vocations that it was seemingly impossible to bring them together, hence but little was done on the occasion. A few of the neighbors were invited, and a supper was given by William and Mary. At the request of some of the guests, I made a short talk on the occasion. Having spent some time in conversation, singing and prayer were had and the company adjourned. My health was bad nearly all the time I remained here, consequently I neither lectured or preached. The Annual Conference at Reidsville having adjourned, Bascom came to see us and requested us to go home with him to his work on the Dobson circuit, so we left here on the 21st of Dec., and on Christmas eve the 24th we arrived at Dobson. On the following Sunday I preached a Christmas sermon, and also on the next Sabbath a New Year's sermon. We continued here about four months, during which time I delivered a course of lectures at Dobson, taught a Grammar class at night, and preached several times at different appointments on his work. On the 30th of April 1887, we left Dobson with a view to visit Victor, Mrs. Rheim, and Mrs. Clontz, our children beyond the Blue Ridge. We spent Sunday, 1st of May at Elkin. I preached in the morning and Bascom at night. I also delivered a lecture on the "Problem of Social Life" on Monday night. Tuesday morning we left for Moravian Falls, where I lectured at night. The next day we reached our son's, at York Institute. I preached on Sunday the 8th in Rocky Springs Church, and lectured on the following Wednesday night on "The Problem of Social Life," and on the following Sunday, the 15th, I preached on the occasion of the Childrens Day, and on Thursday, the 19th we left. Spent the same night with my daughter, Rachel Elliotte, and on the next day we went to Statesville, took the train for Connelly's Springs. Stopping here we were pleasantly domiciled with brother William Connelly. On the next day we attended a Sunday School Pic-Nic at the College. On the next day Sunday 22, I preached at the College twice, and on Monday night lectured on "Education, Man the Proper Subject and End." On Wednesday the 25th we went aboard for Asheville. There we were met by Victor. Spent the night in town, and next day reached Brevard, a distance of 35 or 40 miles. On the Friday following had the pleasure of meeting brother Camell (?) P. E. of the Asheville District, and two other preachers, bros Pickett and Grier. I preached at night, and on the following day we went to a Quarterly Conference of the Blue Ridge Mission, at Greenwood, eight miles distant. At the request of the P. E., I preached on Saturday at 11 and also on Sunday at the same hour. I continued with Victor on his work until the first of September; generally preaching twice on Sunday and some time during the week. Early in this month I reached Prof. Rheim's in Yancey County, where I met with Mrs.York who had left some six weeks before, where we continued here several weeks. But my health was so bad I only preached once, and then had to sit part of the time while preaching. Some time in October we went to Buncombe County to visit my daughter, Mrs. Dr. Clontz. My health had somewhat improved, so that I preached some three times while here. Early in November we left for our old home at York Institute, in Alexander County. Stopping at Connelley's Springs, we spent three days and I preached on Sunday. On the 16th Nov. reached our destination. Here we continued till early in March '88. During the time I taught a class in Grammar and Applied Arithmetic.

Preached on Thanksgiving day and almost every Sunday while here. The congregation was large and appreciative. On Christmas eve we were severely "pounded" by these kind people. In truth we were amply supplied during our stay, and they were exceedingly loath to give us up. On the day before Christmas we were startled with the sad news that our daughter Mrs. T. F. Elliotte, of Iredell County, had on that morning suddenly died, on that morning in the bed. If anyone should enquire how she died, we would say as she had lived a devoted Christian, we have no doubt but that she was ready when the summons came. In this community I had preached to this people more or less for forty years, had taught Grammar and Elocution here more than forty years ago, and subsequently ran a High School for several years. Here Camp-meetings have been held annually for more than fifty years. The church is now in a flourishing condition, and pays nearly $200 yearly to the support of the pastor. It was highly gratifying to us to meet with so much kindness and aid from this people with whom we had in former years spent so much time and labor, even from the noon of life to its dusky eve. While at this place, I visited Taylorsville. Preached on Sunday morning in the Presbyterian church to a large and appreciative congregation, and in the Methodist church at night, and delivered a public lecture in the former church on Monday night. The public manifested their appreciation of my preaching and lecturing by contributing some 12 or 13 dollars. I also preached at Cedar Run to a large audience, at the request of the Principals. Having wound up here we left on the 7th of March to visit Bascom at Big Lick in Stanley County and were met by him on the 8th at Concord, and on the 10 March, 1888, reached this place and found all well.

www.ingramcontent.com/pod-product-compliance
Lightning Source LLC
Chambersburg PA
CBHW051411070526
44584CB00023B/3383